# CHRISTMAS TRADITIONS

## *From the Heart*
### *Volume Two*

## by Margaret Peters

*Christmas joy is in my heart*

**C&T** PUBLISHING

Copyright © 1994 Margaret Peters
Edited by Harold Nadel
Technical information edited by Barbara Kuhn
Design and layout Rose Sheifer/Graphic Productions, Walnut Creek, California
Technical illustrations by Janet White, Walnut Creek, California
Photography by Sharon Risedorph, San Francisco, California
Room styling assistance by Candy MacPherson

Berol Prismacolor is a registered trademark of Empire Berol U.S.A.
Ewe and Me is a registered trademark of Ewe and Me
(325 Lancaster Road, Walnut Creek, CA 94595; telephone 510-934-1895).
Fray Check is a trademark of Dritz Corporation.
Heirloom is a registered trademark of Hobbs Bonded Fibers.
Lycra is a trademark of E.I. du Pont de Nemours and Company.
Mylar is a registered trademark of E. I. duPont de Nemours & Co.
Pigma Micron is a trademark of Sakura Color Products Corporation.
Pilot is a registered trademark of the Pilot Pen Corporation of America.
Soft Touch is a registered trademark of Fairfield Processing.
Stencil-ease and Fab-Tex are registered trademarks of Stencil-ease.
Sulky is a registered trademark of Sulky of America.
Totally Stable is a brand name of Sulky of America.
Wonder Under is a trademark of Pellon Division, Freudenberg Nonwovens.
X-Acto is a registered trademark of Hunt Manufacturing Company.

Library of Congress Cataloging-in-Publication Data
(Revised for vol. 2)

Peters, Margaret, 1931-
    Christmas traditions from the heart.
    Two folded patterns bound in.
    1. Christmas decorations.   2. Patchwork—Patterns  3. Christmas cookery.  4. Needlework—
Patterns.   I. Title.
TT900.C4P455   1992                       745.594 ' 12                       92-71399
    ISBN  0-914881-48-5  (v. 1)
    ISBN  0-914881-79-5  (v. 2)

Published by C & T Publishing
P. O. Box 1456
Lafayette, California 94549

Printed in Hong Kong
10  9  8  7  6  5  4  3  2  1

# CONTENTS

Margaret Peters:
*Treetop Angel and Ornament* ......................................... 5

Gerry Kimmel:
*Trees Around the World* ............................................. 12

Shirley Botsford:
*Christmas Carole* ................................................... 20

Laura Nownes & Lavender Bags:
*Double Nine-Patch Quilt* ........................................... 34

Paul Pilgrim:
*Oh Holy Night Wall Hanging* ........................................ 37

Diana McClun:
*Christmas Table Setting* ........................................... 65

Yvonne Porcella:
*Jewel-Tone Silk Christmas Vest* .................................... 67

Molly Milligan-Cokeley:
*Father Christmas* .................................................. 71

Nicki Becker:
*Folk Art Santa Stocking* ........................................... 85

Cathie I. Hoover:
*Whimsical Cow Christmas Tree Skirt* ................................ 89

Jean Wells:
*Christmas Mini-Socks and Tree Skirt* ............................... 94

Rose Sheifer:
*Holiday Letter and Recipe Cards* ................................... 99

# DEDICATION

*This book is dedicated to my husband, Pete, who has always held my hand through life's scary moments, has never lost faith in me, and is always there;*

*to my dear friend and editor, Harold Nadel, who makes my prose readable;*

*to Rose Sheifer, whose artistic talents bring the sparkle;*

*to Barbara Kuhn, whose magical insight ensures that all these projects work perfectly and easily;*

*and, especially, to Todd and Tony Hensley, who have made all of this possible.*

*Hugs to each of you.*

# MARGARET PETERS

## Treetop Angel and Ornament

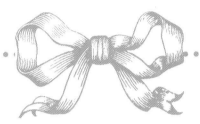

*Before Margaret could stop him, her editor took the initiative to introduce her to you. Since you already know her first book,* Christmas Traditions from the Heart, *you know the basic facts: her bubbling personality, her years as a sales representative for crafts designers and manufacturers, her bubbling personality, her lecturing career, her overflowing love of her thousand Best Friends, her bubbling personality, her home which is a pilgrimage site for antiquers at Christmas and July Fourth, her bubbling personality and, of course, her experiences in designing a Christmas tree for the Smithsonian Institution and an angel ornament for the White House collection— national treasures which we persuaded her to share with you in this book. Reading what she has written about others, you know why she is America's Sweetheart, the author who can get away with calling her editor at eleven at night and then again eight hours later, who leaves messages on his answering machine beginning, "Pick up the phone, Dear Heart: it's me!" (Just a few minutes ago—I swear—another of my authors called me: "Are you on the phone with Margaret?* <u>Both</u> *her call-waiting lines are busy! Give the rest of us a chance to share her.") I'm so glad that I'm her Best Friend, since she is mine.*

Τhe thrill and honor of my life came in 1987, when I was invited to design a Christmas tree for the Smithsonian Institution. This experience changed the direction of my life, bringing me further evidence of the American dream, of the Land of Opportunity. In spite of the popularity of my kits for small angels, I always resisted requests for the treetop angel in a kit—but I couldn't resist giving you the pattern and directions in this book. I have made her here of Christmas fabrics, but I certainly wouldn't be offended if you opt for red, white, and blue.

# Treetop Angel

## Materials Needed

- ¾ yard of muslin for dress
- ⅛ yard each of 2 different Christmas fabrics for hearts on dress
- ⅛ yard of another Christmas fabric for arms
- Two 5" x 4" pieces of solid fabric for heart in angel's hand
- Four 3" x 2" pieces of flesh-colored fabric for hands
- Two 10" x 8" pieces of 2 co-ordinating fabrics (1 solid) for heart wings
- 9" x 9" square of extra-light batting for wings
- ⅓ yard of fusible backing for hearts
- 11" x 17" piece of firm paper or Mylar®
- 2½"-diameter wooden ball with a flat side for head
- 2 packages of Ewe and Me® curly roving
- Three ⅛"-diameter gold beads
- 20" of ⅛"-wide red satin ribbon
- 18" of ¼"-wide red grosgrain ribbon
- Small amount of stuffing for arms and heart in her hands
- 12"-tall foam cone with 5"-diameter base for body
- Spool of gold metallic thread
- Straight scissors (and scalloping shears, optional)
- Water-soluble or disappearing pen
- Black permanent fine-line marking pen
- Strong thread or dental floss
- Hot glue gun

## Assembly Instructions

1. Trace the pattern pieces onto firm paper or Mylar. (The plastic from a package of bacon also works very well!) The arm and hand patterns include the ¼" seam allowances. Use ¼" seam allowance when sewing all the patterns together.

2. Following the manufacturer's directions, apply fusible backing to the wrong sides of the two Christmas fabrics you have chosen for the hearts on the skirt. Trace six small hearts onto each piece of fabric: mark the lines on the paper backing to see them more easily. Cut out the hearts and remove the paper backing.

3. Cut a piece of muslin 42½" x 24½" and press. Beginning ¼" away from one short edge, lay the hearts side by side along one long edge of the muslin, alternating the heart fabrics. The points of the hearts should be ¼" from the long edge and should just touch each other at their sides.

4. Press the hearts onto the skirt bottom. Cut a scalloped edge ¼" from the bottom of the hearts. With the disappearing pen, draw a light line 2" above the hearts and write your Christmas phrase with the permanent pen. (You will want to try this first on a piece of paper the proper length, to work out the spacing.) When writing, keep the fabric taut, use a light touch, and keep the pen moving. On the Christmas angel, I wrote: "Hark, the herald angels sing, Glory to the new-born King! Peace on Earth and Mercy mild, God and sinners reconciled. Hallelujah!" and my name and the date. On the patriotic angel I wrote the Pledge of Allegiance to the Flag. Be sure to sign and date your work, and to add any other pertinent information.

5. Sew the back seam, right sides facing and using ¼" seam allowance, then turn right side out and press. At the end opposite the hearts, turn edge to right side ¼", press, and turn the pressed edge to right side again ¼". Press and then stitch, making a hem on the right side of the skirt. Fold the hemmed side to the inside, to the point where the hearts touch. Press the folded edge: this upper part becomes the bodice.

6. With the disappearing pen, lightly mark lines about every inch, beginning ⅜" down from the fold. Then repeat 1" down from that line, and yet again. You now have 3 light lines for gathering. With very strong thread or white dental floss, gather along those lines.

7. Lower the skirt over the foam cone until the points of the hearts are even with the bottom of the cone. Pull the gathering threads tight and tie them off. The top of the cone will extend above the bodice. Tie the ⅛"-wide ribbon around the neck on top of the first

gathering line, with the knot in the center front. Tie a 1½" bow atop the knot and decoratively arrange the ribbon tails, holding them in place with a dot of hot glue (a tooth-pick helps). Hot glue the gold beads to the center front of the gathering lines.

8. Cut out four arms and four hands from the chosen fabrics. Lay a hand on the right side of an arm, as shown on the pattern, and sew only across the hand; repeat for all four. Press the hand out to the front of the arm. Put two arm pieces together, right sides facing, and sew around the entire arm and hand, leaving an opening where indicated on the pattern. Clip the curves and turn. Stuff the arm gently to give it shape. Whipstitch the opening closed. Repeat for the other arm.

9. Cut two small hearts, using the same heart pattern for her dress, from the solid fabric. Write "Peace" or "Joy" on the center of one heart and place the two together, right sides facing; sew around them, leaving a small opening for turning. Clip curves, then turn and stuff the heart slightly. Whipstitch the opening closed.

10. Hold one arm against the body, a little behind the shoulder, and determine the best place-ment: remember that you will be folding the arm to hold the heart. Hot glue both arms to the body. Place the heart in the hands, with the arms bent, and hot glue the heart to the hands.

11. Cut one package of roving into three equal lengths; the specific length is unimportant right now. Remove the strings and fluff the hair until you like the look. Two pieces will be for the sides, and one for the top and back. Run hot glue onto the ball, keeping one section clear for the face, and glue the hair in place with light pressure. Take the second package of braided hair and, beginning 5" from one end (the 5" will form a tress), glue the braid to the center back of the head (this is your starting point). Hot glue the braid around her head, dipping down to her ears, leaving enough hair showing in front for bangs, and ending at the center back of the head. You should have at least 5" of remaining braid for

another tress. Pull the braids out of the tresses. Cut the center strings where the braids join at the back of the head, and pull them out. Tie the tresses together with a knot where the braids join, using the ¼"-wide ribbon. Tie the ribbon into a 3" bow atop the knot.

12. Cut one Wing Heart #1 from the solid wing fabric, preferably with scalloping shears. With straight scissors, cut one Wing Heart #2 from batting and one from the Christmas fabric. Trim a scant ⅛" off the edges of the batting so it will not protrude. Baste the 3 layers together, right sides out, and crisscross the center several times. You can now quilt the wing by hand or machine, with metallic thread, around the motifs in the fabric, or use stipple quilting. Remove the basting threads and hot-glue the wing down the center of the angel's back, solid fabric facing out.

13. Cut off the remainder of the cone even with the top of the dress. Run hot glue on the flat side of the head and attach it to the top of the cone. Arrange the hair over her shoulders and in the back. Trim the hair to the length you prefer, remembering that the sides go in front of her wings and the back hangs over the heart.

14. To place the angel on the tree, I used an apple corer to carve a hole 3" to 4" deep in the center of the cone. If the hole is too large, the angel will wobble. Push it down onto the top branches to steady it.

# Angel Ornament

## Materials Needed

- 12" x 6" piece of muslin for body
- 5" x 7" piece of Christmas fabric for arms
- Two 5" x 4" squares of 2 co-ordinating fabrics (1 solid) for heart wings
- 5" x 4" piece of fusible backing for wing
- 8" x 11" piece of firm paper or Mylar
- 25mm wooden bead for head
- Package of Ewe and Me curly roving
- Small tree, star, bell, or other trinket for angel to hold

- 16" of translucent fishing line
- Small amount of stuffing for arms and body
- Straight scissors (and scalloping shears, optional)
- Black permanent fine-line marking pen
- Hot glue gun

## Assembly Instructions

1. Trace the pattern pieces onto firm paper or Mylar. The body and arm pieces include the ¼" seam allowances. Use ¼" seam allowance when sewing all the patterns together.

2. Trace the body and arm patterns onto the chosen fabrics, aligning the pieces on the fabric folds, and cut.

3. Lay out the muslin body, right side up. Write your Christmas phrase on the left side of the body. When writing, keep the fabric taut, use a light touch, and keep the pen moving.

4. Fold the body in half, right sides facing. Sew together at the top and bottom, leaving openings where indicated on the pattern. Do not sew along the fold. Backstitch for stability at the ends. Turn and stuff gently to give it shape. Whipstitch the bottom opening closed.

5. Fold the arm pieces in half, right sides facing, and sew together. Leave a small opening on the lower edge, as indicated on the pattern. Backstitch as needed, clip corner, and turn. Stuff lightly. Whipstitch the opening closed.

6. Following the manufacturer's directions, apply the fusible backing to the wrong side of the fabric you have chosen for the wing. Trace Wing Heart #3 onto the paper backing and cut out. Remove the paper backing. Center the heart atop the solid fabric and fuse them together. Cut around the heart, leaving a ¼" border. You can use scalloping shears for a whimsical touch.

7. Fold the heart wing in half, solid sides facing, and whipstitch the fold to the angel's back. A dot of hot glue in the center will hold the wings upright.

8. Make pen dots for eyes, just above the middle of the wooden bead.

9. Cut 3" of the roving, but do not unbraid it. Twist one end of the hair, in a screwing

motion, about ¼" into the top of the bead. Unbraid the hair and remove the strings.

10. Turn the muslin at the neck edge inside ¼". Stuff to the neck line. Run hot glue around the inside of the neck fabric and place the head, gathering the fabric around the head.

11. Hot glue the arms to the shoulders, making sure the fronts of the arms are even. Glue the trinket into her hands. Separate and fluff the hair, and trim it to the desired length. Lift the hair and apply hot glue at the sides and back of the head, then press the hair in place gently to frame her face.

12. To place the angel on the tree, tie the ends of the fishing line together to make a loop. Bring the loop around the front of the angel's chest, placing the line under her arms, so the angel will hang evenly.

❤ I have learned of some interesting family traditions which people have developed using my angel ornaments. One woman told me that she made six angels, for herself, her husband, and their four children. On the back of the children's she wrote the name, birth date, and birthplace; on the adults' she wrote their wedding date. On Christmas morning, she places the angel on each person's breakfast plate, for hanging on the tree. Another woman ordered 22 kits: she was corresponding with 22 service personnel fighting in Desert Storm, and was sending a Guardian Angel to each. The world is indeed full of wonderful people, angels on Earth.

In my own family, one of our Christmas traditions developed several years ago, at Thanksgiving. To get our two sons to turn off the television and stop eating everything in the house before dinner, I suggested in front of their children that it would be fun to start decorating the house for Christmas. My sons tried to resist, but the grandchildren voted with me. As we began pulling treasures from the cupboards and arranging them, my sons announced that the nativity scene had been put in the "wrong place"; from then on, it was a family project. Although the living room became a shambles, with Christmas appearing and all the displaced objects piling up, we did abandon the television, work up appetites for Thanksgiving dinner, and create a new tradition. Every year since, the grandchildren have been ready to start decorating,

and we have one more reason to be thankful that we are together. I remember my mother telling me, "Have fun with your children now; they will be this small for only fifteen minutes." She was wrong: it's only five minutes, or less, so begin your own family traditions now.

For many years when our children were young, they decorated the sliding glass door in our family room: Dirk or Dianne drew the outlines in tempera, then Mary or Scott filled in the colors. The theme changed each year, ranging from snowmen to the Holy Family. Most popular of all was the year of the Peanuts characters decorating their Christmas tree.

Since the painting was on the inside of the glass, it could stay up all month. It was a fun project that involved the whole family, not just the painting but also the planning for the next year's creation. I remember those days so fondly that I think next Thanksgiving would be a good time to renew the tradition, with our grandchildren.

Our family has had this bread on Christmas morning for as long as I can remember. The recipe goes back at least as far as my great-grandmother, who was born 140 years ago. My grandmother wrote it down in 1910, in a ledger I treasure; it includes the cost of many of the meals.

# Grandma Ragland's Orange Bread

### (makes 2 loaves)

Remove the peels from 6 oranges. Boil them until tender (about 20 minutes), drain, and cut into thin slices (julienne). I change the water 3 times during the cooking, to remove any bitterness.

Make a syrup of 2 cups of sugar and 1 cup of water. Add the peel and cook until the syrup is absorbed and the peel is transparent.

Mix together well
4 cups of flour
3 teaspoons of baking powder
1 cup of sugar
1 teaspoon of salt
¼ cup of shortening
1 cup of milk
2 eggs, thoroughly beaten.

Add the cooked peel to this dough. Place the mixture in a greased bread pan and let it stand 20 minutes. Then bake at 350° for one hour. As soon as you remove the bread from the oven, wrap it in a towel. It is best to leave it wrapped for several days before cutting.

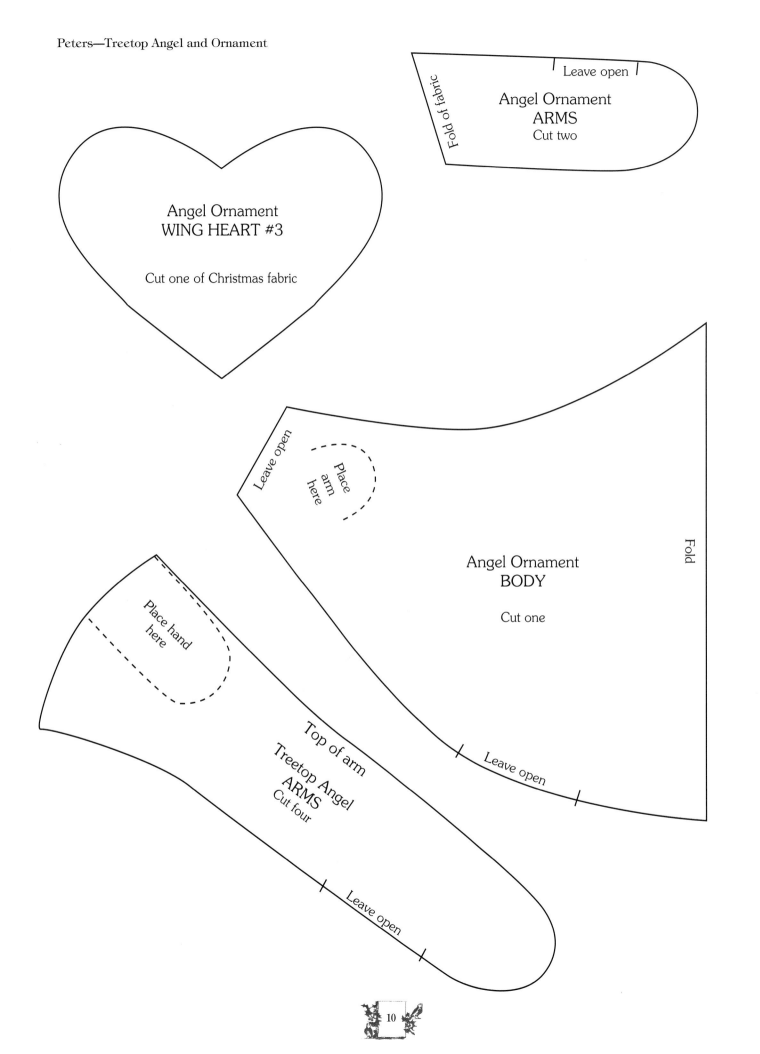

Angel Ornament
ARMS
Cut two

Fold of fabric

Leave open

Angel Ornament
WING HEART #3

Cut one of Christmas fabric

Leave open

Place
arm
here

Angel Ornament
BODY

Cut one

Fold

Leave open

Place hand
here

Top of arm
Treetop Angel
ARMS
Cut four

Leave open

Leave open

10

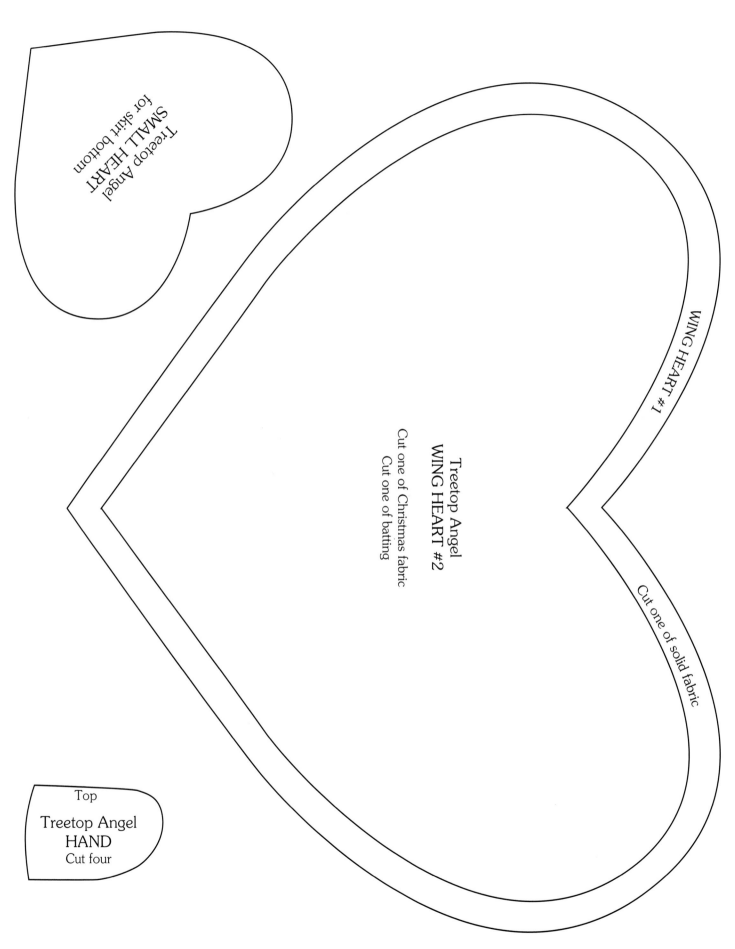

Treetop Angel
SMALL HEART
for skirt bottom

Treetop Angel
WING HEART #2
Cut one of Christmas fabric
Cut one of batting

WING HEART #1

Cut one of solid fabric

Top
Treetop Angel
HAND
Cut four

# GERRY
# KIMMEL

## Trees Around the World

Gerry Kimmel has been my friend since my days as a sales representative. She is owner, editor, publisher, and designer for Red Wagon, one of my favorite companies: she specializes in American primitives, the style that most touches my soul. Her shop in Liberty, Missouri, was a quilter's dream; although she sold it two years ago, she assures me that it remains the same. Her love of life and her positive attitude, along with her deep spirituality, are inspiring and contagious. Like most of the top designers in the quilting world, her generosity is unlimited: one of my greatest thrills in compiling these books is the chance to introduce you to talented and wonderful friends like Gerry.

Finished size 80" x 90"

## Materials Needed

- ½ yard each of 6 or 7 blue plaids
- ½ yard each of 5 or 6 red plaids or prints
- ⅝ yard of blue plaid for top border
- ⅝ yard of blue plaid for right border
- 1½ yards of blue plaid for bottom and left borders
- ¼ yard each of 6 to 8 green plaids or prints for trees
- ⅞ yard for binding

## Assembly

*You must add ¼" seam allowance to the templates.*

Assemble Block A as shown. Attach block borders (patterns 2 and 3) to each side of the center (pattern 1). Add block borders (patterns 4 and 5) to the other sides. Make 31 of Block A, using a variety of fabrics.

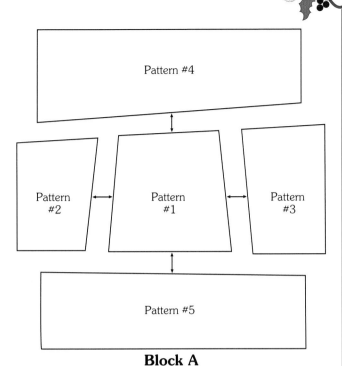

**Block A**

Assemble Block B as shown. Attach block border (pattern 7) to the center (pattern 6). Add block borders (patterns 8 and 9) to this unit, then add block border (pattern 10). Make 22 of Block B, using a variety of fabrics.

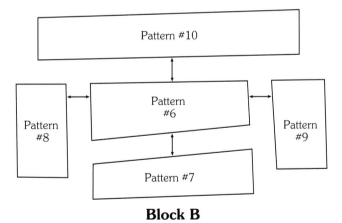

**Block B**

Assemble the quilt top, turning the blocks, as shown.

*The following measurements do include seam allowances.*

For the top border, cut a strip 60½" x 10½"; this can be pieced. Using a variety of trees (patterns 11-15) and of fabrics, cut 8 trees and appliqué them to the strip. Attach the strip to the top of the quilt. Add ornaments (pattern 16) to some of the trees, using the color photograph as a guide. Attach to the top of the quilt.

For the right border, cut (and piece) a strip 80½" x 10½". Add 10 trees and ornaments in the same manner, and attach to the right side of the quilt.

For the bottom border, cut (and piece) a strip 70½" x 10½". Add 9 trees and ornaments, and attach to the bottom of the quilt.

For the left border, cut (and piece) a strip 90½" x 10½". Add 11 trees and ornaments, and attach to the left side of the quilt.

Add batting, backing, and binding. I have done outline and echo quilting around the blocks and trees.

❤ Each year, my family tries to prepare foods from different cultures—Greek baklava, Italian cannoli, Indian curry, etc.—to remind us that we are all the same in the eyes of God and that all peoples can celebrate the peace which is Christmas.

# Gingerbread Cookies

1 cup of sugar
2 tsp. ginger
1 tsp. cinnamon
1 tsp. nutmeg
½ tsp. salt
1½ tsp. baking soda

Combine above and mix well. Add:

1 cup of melted margarine
½ cup of evaporated milk
1 cup of dark molasses
½ tsp. vanilla extract

Mix well and add:
4 to 4½ cups of flour, a little at a time. Knead dough until smooth. Roll dough to ¼" thick on a floured surface and cut into cookies. Bake on a greased cookie sheet for 9 to 11 minutes at 375°. Cookies are done if they spring back when touched. Makes 2 dozen.

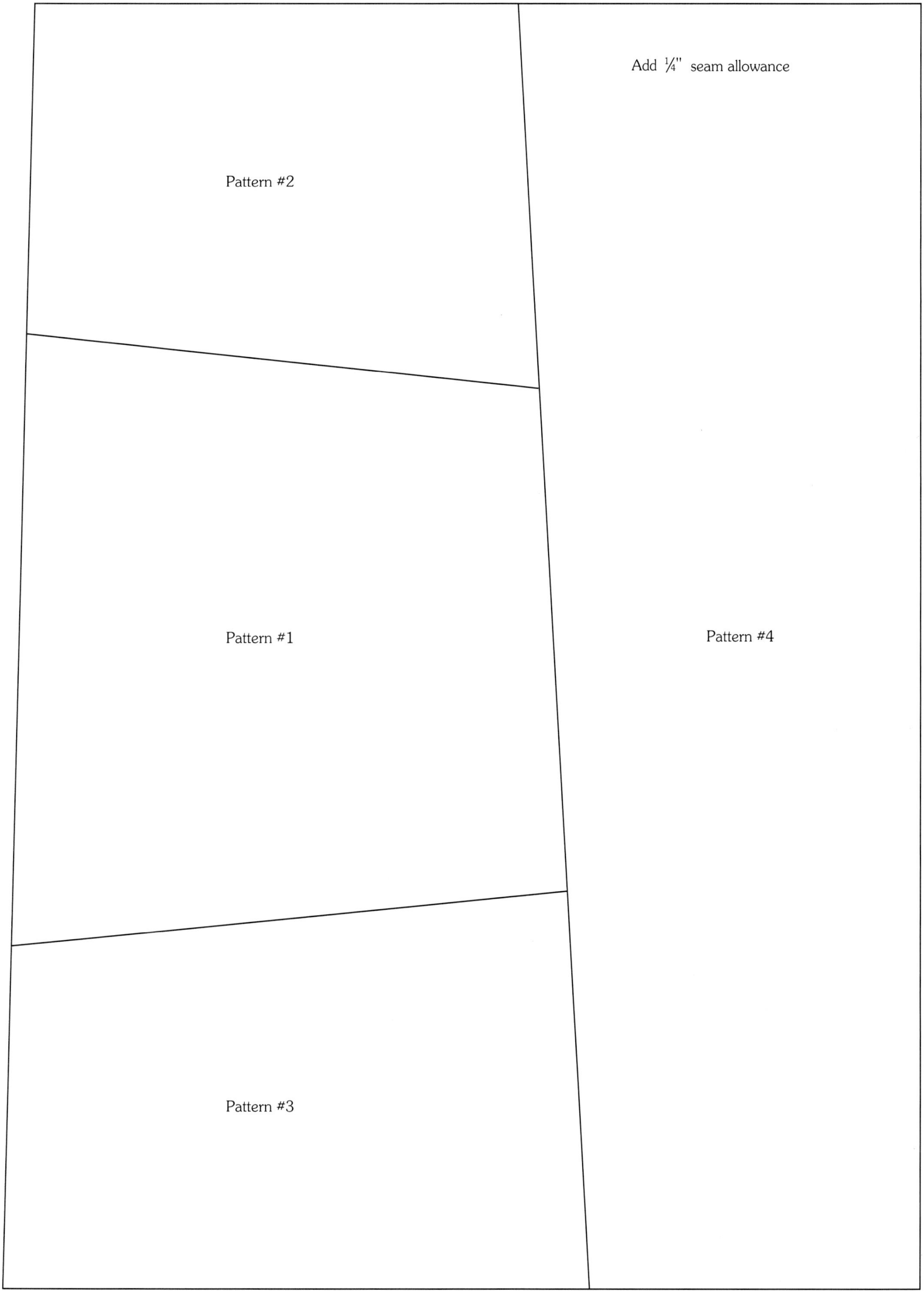

Pattern #2

Add ¼" seam allowance

Pattern #1

Pattern #4

Pattern #3

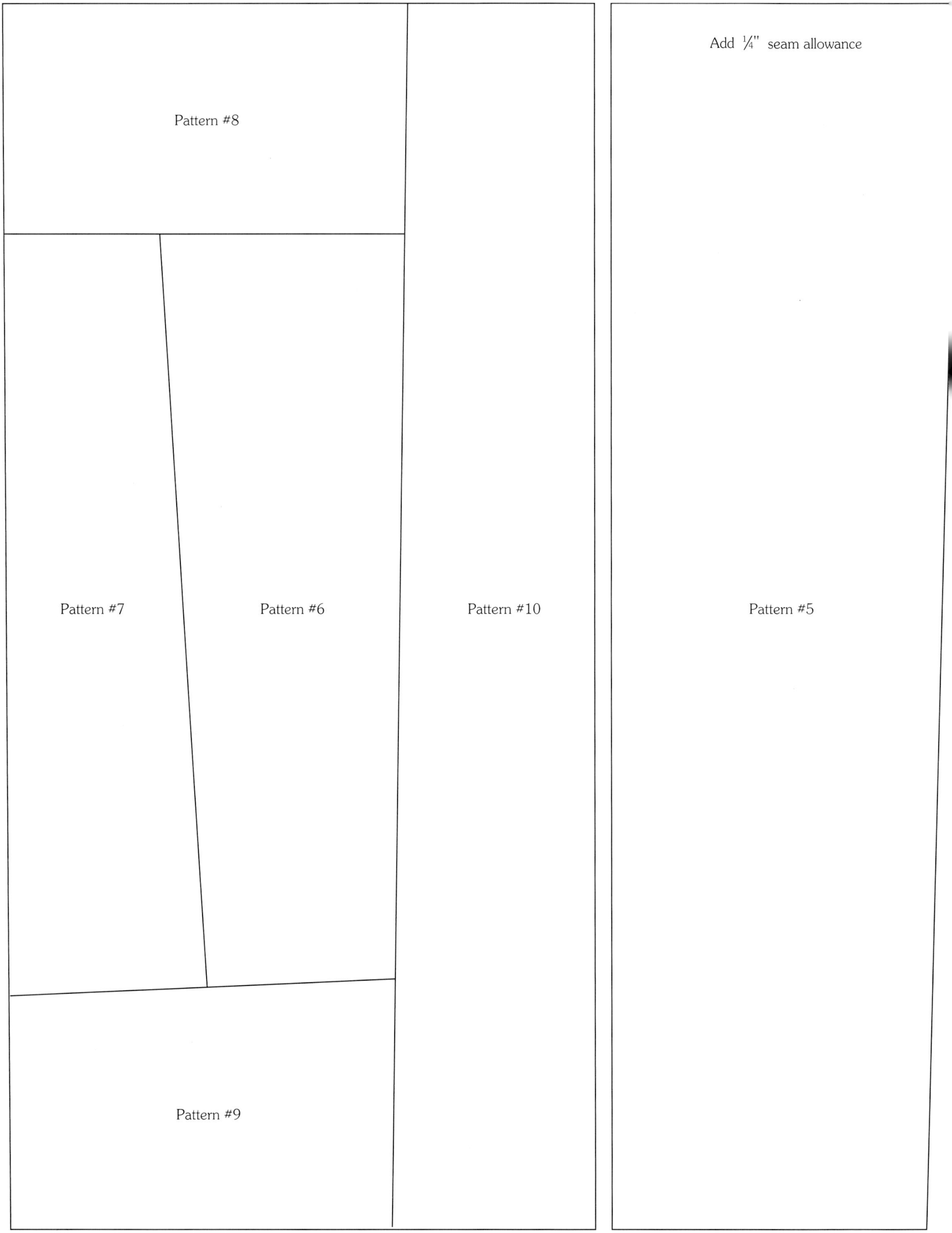

Pattern #8

Add ¼" seam allowance

Pattern #7

Pattern #6

Pattern #10

Pattern #5

Pattern #9

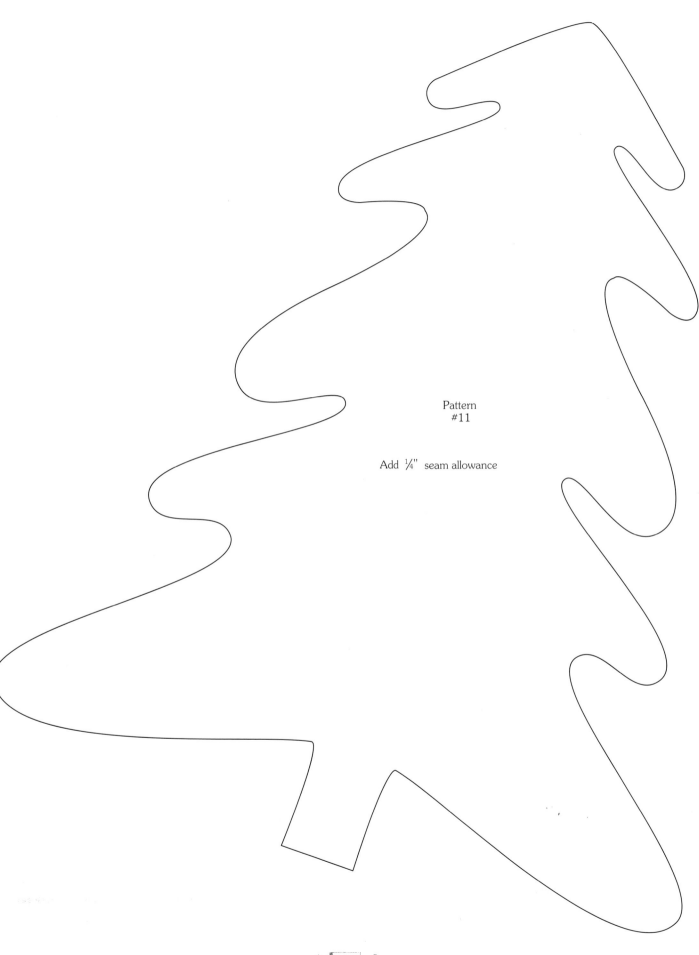

Pattern
#11

Add ¼" seam allowance

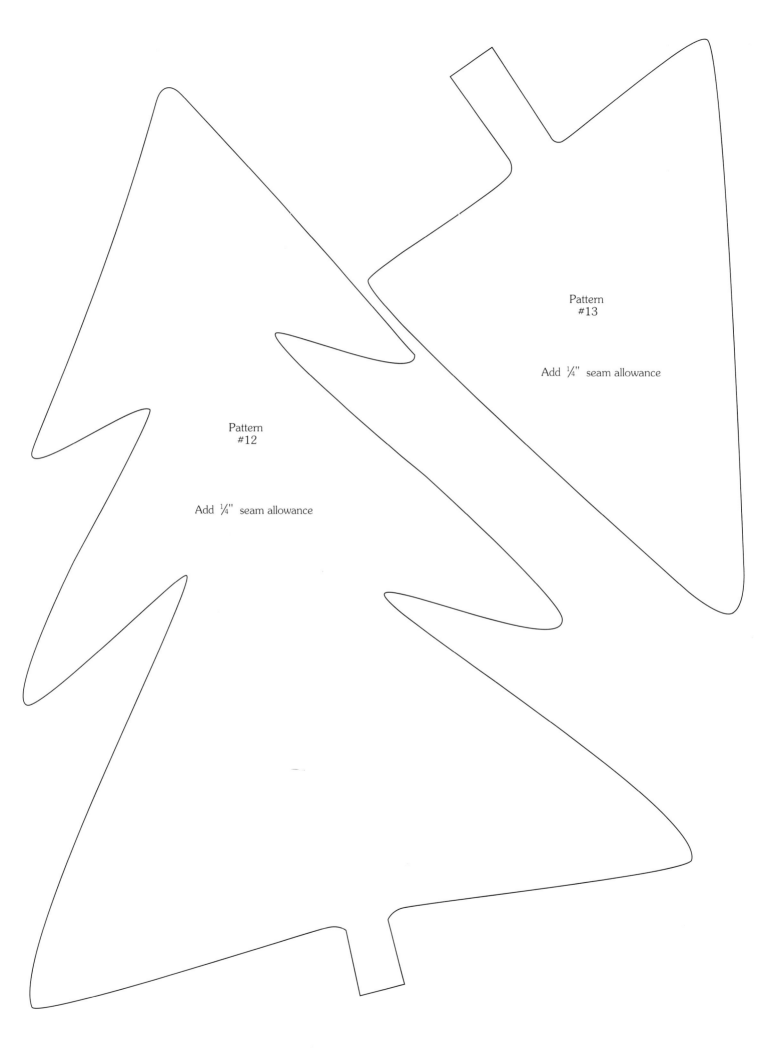

Pattern
#13

Add ¼" seam allowance

Pattern
#12

Add ¼" seam allowance

Pattern #15

Add ¼" seam allowance

Pattern #14

Pattern #16

## Christmas Carole
### a 20" Cloth Doll

Christmas Carole is #140 in the series of doll patterns "Shirley's Girls," designed and marketed exclusively by Shirley Botsford.

### Doll Materials

- Peach broadcloth—½ yard
- Bright red wool roving—5 packages
- Co-ordinating thread for fabric and roving
- Template cardboard
- Stuffing
- Knitting needle
- Disappearing ink pen
- Fabric paints—red, blue, black, brown, white
- Fine-tipped fabric paint brush
- Pink chalk
- White glue

### Clothing Materials

- Ivory satin for pantaloons and blouse—⅝ yard
- Ivory embroidered 1"-wide lace trim—1 yard
- Elastic ¼"-wide—½ yard
- Three snaps
- Burgundy lightweight brocade for skirt—⅞ yard
- Gold ¼"-wide picot trim—1 yard
- Black vinyl for belt—⅛ yard
- Belt buckle
- Green taffeta for bonnet—⅞ yard
- Ivory bonnet lace, 1¾" (pre-gathered)—⅜ yard
- Co-ordinating 1½"-wide wire ribbon for bonnet—1 yard
- Cord for bonnet casing—½ yard
- Perfect Pleater™ board (available from Clotilde Inc., 1909 SW First Avenue, Fort Lauderdale, FL 33315-2100)
- Green quilted velvet for coat—¾ yard
- Green lightweight brocade for coat lining—¾ yard
- Green ⅜"-wide braid trim—4 yards

*Shirley Botsford is one of the country's leading designers: crafts projects for several magazines and pattern companies, clothing that has starred in the Fairfield Fashion Show, a line of fabrics, the well-remembered challenge show Accessories As Art. I still smile when I think back on an unforgettable doll she designed; so, too, when I think of Shirley, with her calm, smiling personality and giving nature, filling a room with sunshine.*

- White faux fur—⅓ yard
- Black yarn—1 skein of 3-ply
- Template cardboard
- Co-ordinating sewing threads for clothing materials

## Assembly

### DOLL

1. Tape the pieces of the doll pattern together. Place it on template cardboard and transfer all markings. Then turn it over to complete the other half of the doll, and again transfer all markings. Cut out the template.

2. Fold the peach fabric in half, right sides together, so you are cutting a double layer of fabric. On the wrong side of the fabric, position the doll template on the bias grain. Draw around it with a disappearing ink pen. **Add ¼" seam allowance** and cut out the two doll pieces. Transfer the face and all the markings to the right side of the fabric on the front or back of the doll, as indicated. **Solid lines and dots are for the front of the doll, and open dots are for the back.**

3. Paint the face, using a very fine brush, as follows: eyebrows, nose, chin, and inside of mouth in brown; lips in red; outline of eyes, pupils, and lashes in black; iris of eyes in blue; whites of eyes, highlights on pupils, nose, and lip in white. Allow each color to dry thoroughly before using the next color. Use pink chalk to blush the face if you wish.

4. With right sides together, pin the doll front and back together. Using the smallest stitch on your machine, stitch the front and back together along the template outline. Leave an opening for stuffing, as indicated. Stitch a second time, just ¹⁄₁₆" outside the first stitching.

   Trim the seam allowance to ⅛". Clip to the stitching at the ears, thumbs, neck, underarms, and crotch. Turn the doll right side out. Use a knitting needle to coax open very carefully all the detailed areas. Roll the seam edges out completely between your fingers, and press the doll flat.

5. Place a tiny amount of stuffing in the hands, feet, and ear areas of the doll. Stitch the fingers, toes, and ears right through the stuffing. Knot the thread ends and sink them neatly so they can't be seen. Stuff the arms and head, then stitch the underarm joints. Use a zipper foot if necessary. Next, stuff the sewn leg and stitch that leg joint. Stuff the body and stitch the remaining leg joint. Then stuff the remaining leg. Slip stitch the opening closed.

6. Use a double thread to hand stitch the dimple details on her knees, belly button, elbows, and fanny. Sink the knot into the stuffing and stitch back and forth between the dimples three times. Pull the thread so you make a slight dimple. Knot the thread at a seam, where it will not be noticeable.

7. Undo each length of roving and separate it to a width of about 1½". Cut four 20" lengths. From the scraps of doll fabric, cut a 1" x 7" piece. Press under ½" on each short edge. Center the four 20" lengths on the fabric strip, completely covering it. Machine stitch the roving to the middle of the strip, using matching thread. Fold the hair in one direction and press lightly. Cut three 5" lengths for bangs from the remaining roving. Center them over the previous stitch line, at the middle of the fabric strip. Stitch them to the fabric as before. Fold the long edges of the fabric strip in half and hand stitch it to the doll's head along the seam, between the ears. Apply a light coat of white glue to the back of the doll's head. Arrange the hair down the back of the head, setting it in the glue. Fold the bangs to the front of the face and spot glue if you wish.

### CLOTHES

Use ¼" seam allowance for clothing construction: this is included in the patterns. Trace patterns onto template cardboard, extending pattern lines, if needed, as indicated. Cut out the patterns.

### Pantaloons

Cut 2 pantaloon patterns from the satin. Sew the front and back side seams, right sides together.

Hem the bottom leg edges and apply the embroidered lace trim. Cut two 4½" lengths of elastic. To gather the satin, 2" above the lace trim, zigzag the elastic to the wrong side of the legs. Stitch the inner leg seams. Press the waist edge under ½" for the casing and stitch. Insert a 9" length of elastic, stitch the elastic ends together, close the casing, and turn the pantaloons right side out.

### Blouse

Sew all seams with right sides facing.

Cut an 8" x 10" rectangle from the satin. Make 13 pin tucks in the center of the rectangle. Cut out the blouse front, centering it on the pin tucks. Cut the blouse backs. Sew the shoulder seams together. Cut two sleeves. Hem the wrist edges and apply the embroidered lace trim. Gather the sleeve caps and sew them to the armholes of the blouse. Sew the side underarm seams. Hem the lower edge. Finish the neck edge with the lace trim. Turn under a ½" facing on both back edges. Attach two snaps and turn the blouse right side out.

### Skirt

Cut 2 skirt patterns from the brocade, cutting only one center back facing. Sew the front skirt seam, right sides together. Cut a 1½" x 11" waistband. Cut three 5½" x 44" strips for the ruffle and piece them together. On the bottom edge of the ruffle strip, press under 2¼". On the top edge, press under ¾". Baste all layers together, ½" from the top edge. Pleat the ruffle, following the instructions for the Perfect Pleater. Topstitch the ruffle to the bottom of the skirt along the basted line. Apply the gold trim to cover the stitching. Gather the waist to 9½". With right sides together, fold the waistband in half lengthwise and finish the ends. Turn right side out and press. Sew the back skirt seam, stopping at the dot, as indicated on the pattern. Press the center back facing and finish the opening edges. Sew the waistband to the skirt, allowing a 1" extension on the right back side. Sew the snap in place.

### Belt

Cut a length of vinyl ⅝" x 12" and attach the buckle on one end. Round the other end. Try it on the doll and punch holes in the center of the belt to fit. Cut a ⅝" x 2" length of vinyl for a belt keeper, stitching the short ends together to form a loop. Tack it to the belt at the buckle end.

### Shoes

Cut out the patterns to make a left and right shoe from the vinyl. Overlap the lacer sections over the tongue approximately ¼" on the inner sides, aligning the bottom edges. Place the top curved edge of the toe over the bottom curve of the sections ¼". Topstitch on the right side ⅛" from the edge. With right sides together, stitch the assembled front to the back. Turn the shoe right side out and lace with the yarn.

### Bonnet

Cut a 5" x 20" bonnet back and a 5½" x 32" brim from the taffeta. Fold the brim in half lengthwise and finish the ends. Turn right side out and press. Following the instructions for the Perfect Pleater, pleat the brim to 10". Hem the short ends of the bonnet back piece. Press one long edge under ⅜" to make a casing. Gather the other edge to 10". With right sides together, sew the brim to the gathered edge of the bonnet. Cut the lace to 10½" and hem the ends. Sew the lace to the inside along the brim seam. Tack ribbon over the brim seam on the right side and secure it at both sides of the bonnet. Insert cord through the casing, pulling it up as tightly as possible, and knot the ends. Pass the ribbon behind the doll's head under the hair, and tie the tails into a bow at one side.

### Coat

Sew seams right sides facing, unless otherwise noted.

Cut patterns from the velvet and brocade lining. Sew the shoulder and side seams together on the coat. Sew the shoulder seams together on the cape. Measure all edges of the coat and cape, add ½", then cut the fur strips 2" wide by the edge length. Thread yarn and, working from the front of the fur, insert the needle to the back of the strip, then to the front. Knot the tails and trim them to ½". Apply yarn every 1½" down the center of the fur strips. Matching the edges, sew fur strips to the bottom edges of the cape, coat, and sleeves, and to the

fronts of the coat and cape. Slip stitch the remaining raw edges of the trim to the fabric. Topstitch the green braid to the coat along the inner edges of the fur trim. Sew the lining pieces to the front and bottom edges of the coat and cape, and turn. Sew the lining piece to each sleeve bottom. Understitch the lining by sewing on the right side of the lining through all the layers of the seam allowance, $\frac{1}{8}$" from the seam. Understitching will prevent the lining from protruding past the sleeve hem at the wrist. Baste the lining and the velvet together at the neck and armhole edges; baste the sleeve edges at the sides and armhole; baste the cape at the neck. Sew the underarm sleeve seams. Insert the sleeves. Baste the cape to the coat at the neck edges. Cut a 2" x 9" piece of fur for the collar and add the yarn tails. Fold in half lengthwise, right sides together, and finish the ends. Turn right side out and apply to the neck edge.

## Muff

Cut a $6\frac{1}{2}$" square of fur. Sew two opposite edges together, right sides facing, and turn. Tuck the raw edges into the center of the muff and tack them in place. Add black yarn tails. Tack the muff to the doll's hands.

♥ Making ornaments has always been a tradition in my family. When we were growing up, my mother, Jean Botsford, asked my brother Gary and me to make a new ornament for the tree each year. This has produced some wonderful—and some very silly—ornaments that I still have in my collection. I really think that her motivation was creative in concept, but proved to be very practical as well. Gary and I would spend hours doing—and re-doing—our ornaments before showing them to Mom. They had to be just right and, with six years' difference in our ages, we took lots of time out to compete and to fight over the materials. (I think that this also might have been a clever way to get me to do some free babysitting while my mother did her Christmas shopping.) Whatever the reason, this tradition remains with me today. Each year, I create a special ornament based on a technique that I have just learned, a new product that I've discovered, or simply a unique design that I've been thinking about. I usually start planning the ornament for the next year as soon as Christmas is over. I trade ornaments with a group of friends as our gift exchange. I put up a special tree in my office, just to hold all the handmade keepsake ornaments that I've received over the years. Often I share the instructions for my ornament with a church group so they can make dozens of them for their pre-Christmas fundraising project. A few of my friends duplicate lots of their own ornaments to sell at a Christmas bazaar or open house, for a little extra shopping money. No matter how you use them, it's lots of fun to design your own "signature" ornament each year. Kids can join in and help, too! I find that I can't go anywhere during the holidays without hearing, "So, what's your new ornament this year?"

## Shirley's Own Sausage and Wild Rice Stuffing

Nobody's ever asked me for a recipe before, so you could really be taking a big chance! However, I make this stuffing every year and everyone seems to love it. There's never a spoonful left over, so I guess it's OK to put the recipe in print. Feel free to experiment and add things to it: that's how I developed the recipe in the first place. (Sometimes I add button mushrooms or a grated carrot.)

| | |
|---|---|
| 2 cups of pumpernickel bread cubes | ½ cup of chicken stock |
| 2 cups of French bread cubes | 2 eggs or substitute |
| Medium onion, chopped | ¼ cup of butter or substitute |
| Small green pepper, chopped | 1 tablespoon of olive oil or substitute |
| Two celery stalks, sliced | 1 teaspoon of salt or substitute |
| One pound of sweet Italian sausage | ½ teaspoon of pepper |
| One cup of cooked wild rice | ¼ cup of fresh parsley, chopped |

1. Cook the wild rice according to the package directions to yield one cup after cooking.
2. Remove the sausage from the casings, brown it, and crumble it into small pieces. Drain on paper towels to remove fat.
3. Sauté the onion, green pepper, and celery lightly in one tablespoon of olive oil.
4. Beat the eggs lightly in a large mixing bowl. Add all the other ingredients and mix well.
5. Pack stuffing loosely into your turkey or chicken and roast as you usually do. If you prefer, bake the stuffing in a covered casserole at 325° for 45 minutes.

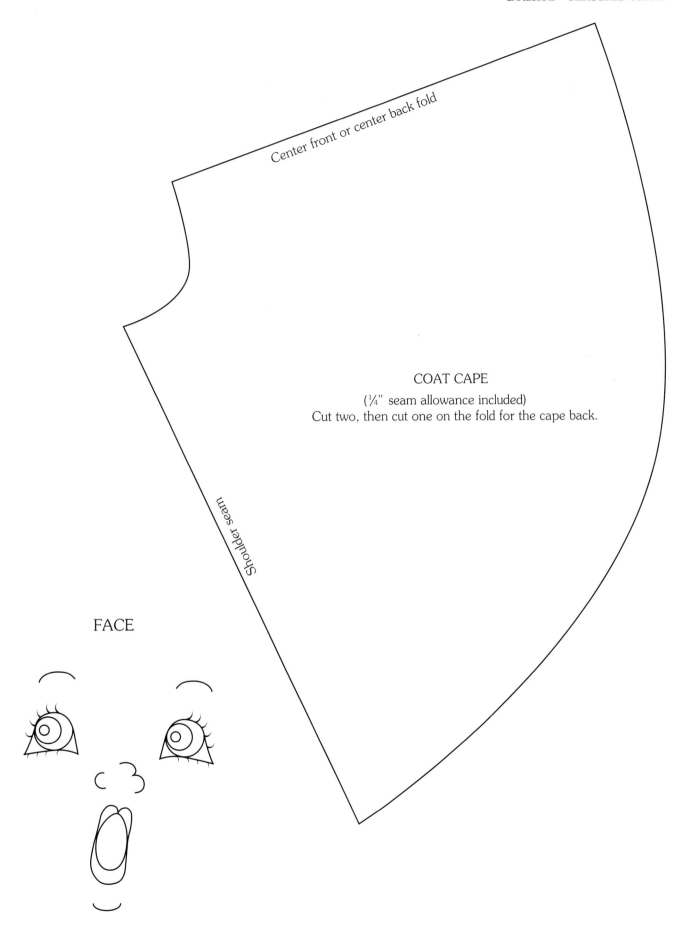

Center front or center back fold

Shoulder seam

COAT CAPE
(¼" seam allowance included)
Cut two, then cut one on the fold for the cape back.

FACE

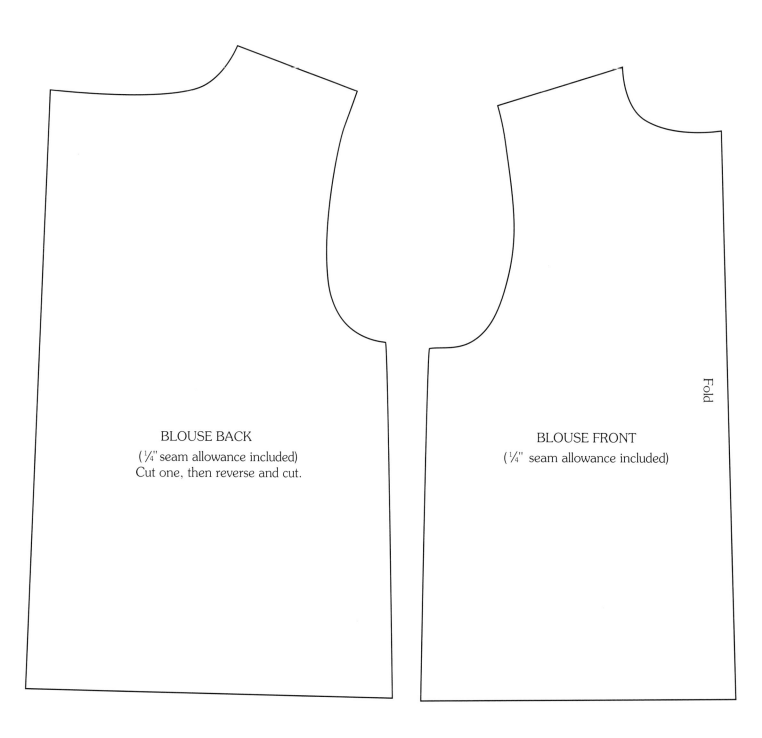

BLOUSE BACK
(¼" seam allowance included)
Cut one, then reverse and cut.

BLOUSE FRONT
(¼" seam allowance included)

Fold

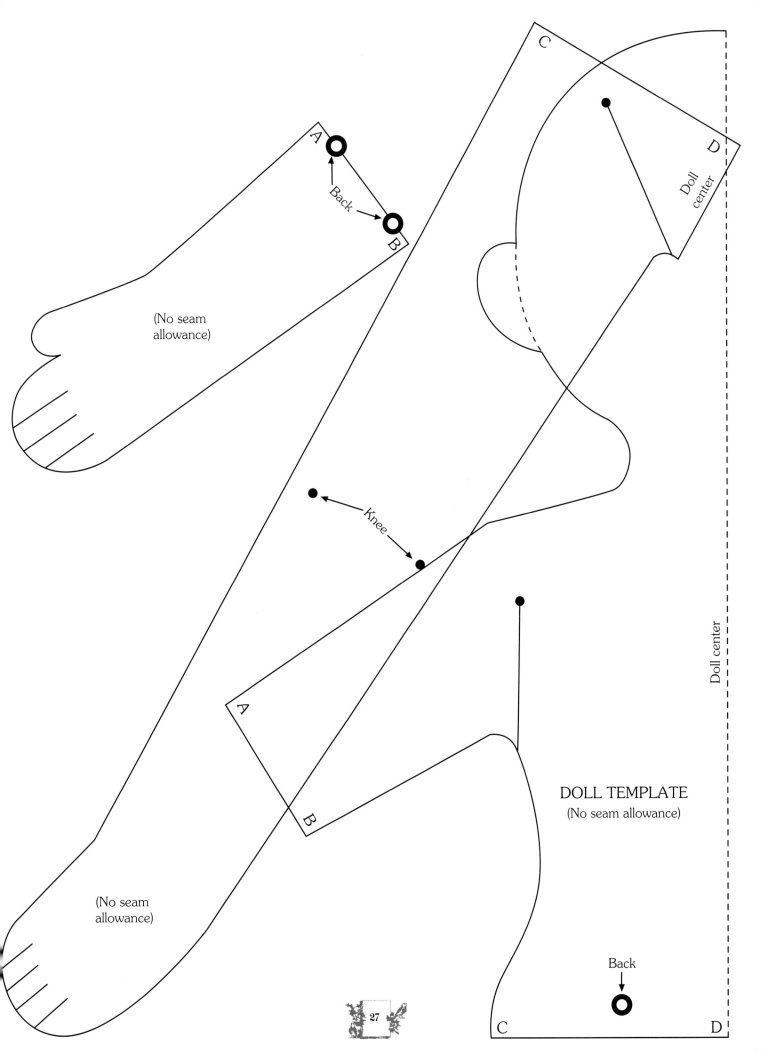

(No seam allowance)

Back

Doll center

Knee

A

B

C

D

Doll center

DOLL TEMPLATE
(No seam allowance)

(No seam allowance)

Back

C

D

27

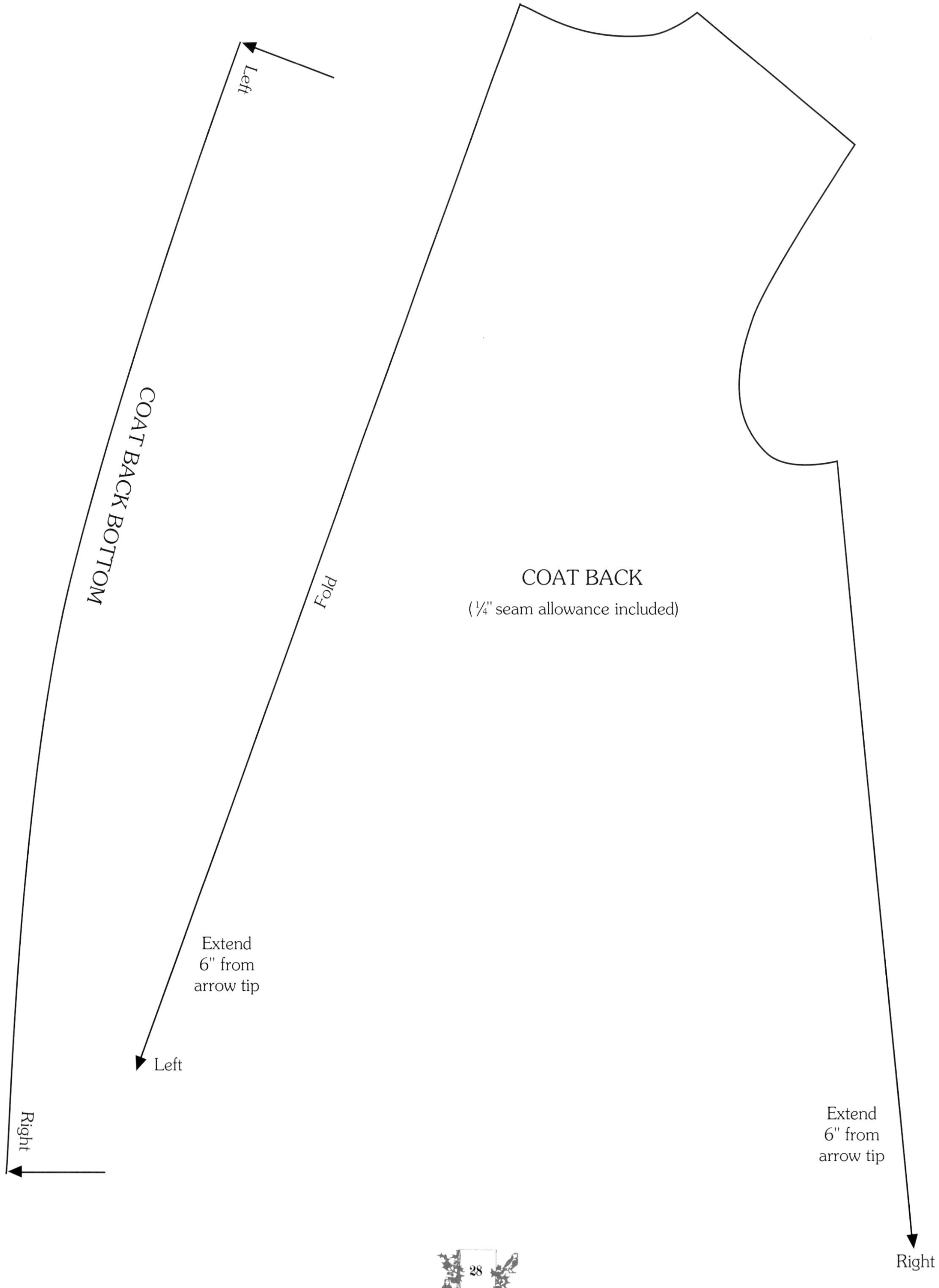

Left

COAT BACK BOTTOM

Fold

COAT BACK

(¼" seam allowance included)

Extend
6" from
arrow tip

Left

Right

Extend
6" from
arrow tip

Right

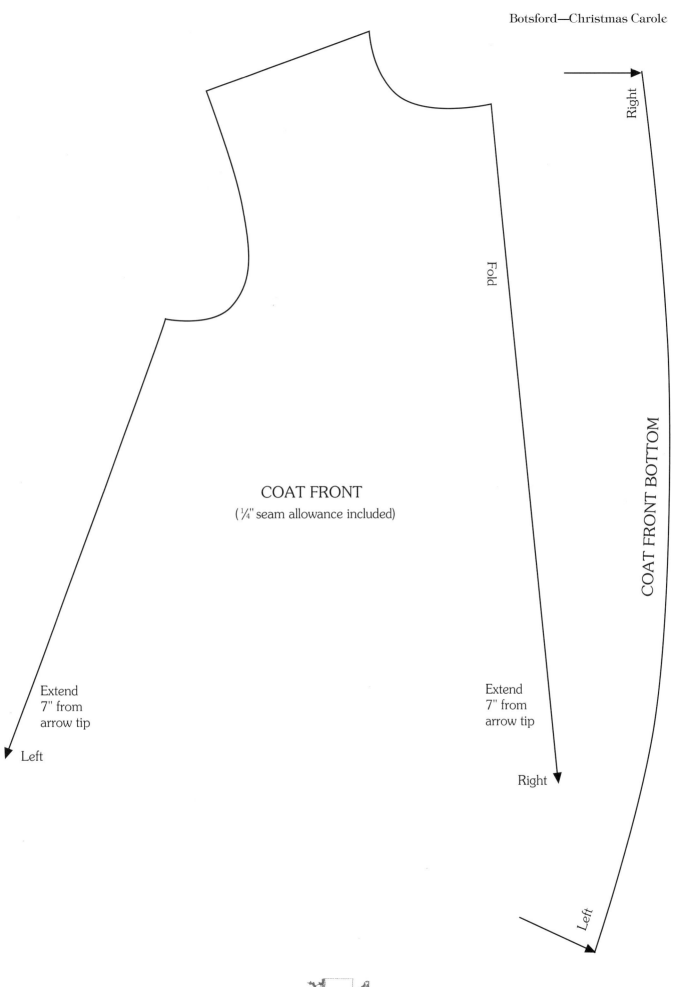

Right

Fold

COAT FRONT

(¼" seam allowance included)

COAT FRONT BOTTOM

Extend
7" from
arrow tip

Left

Extend
7" from
arrow tip

Right

Left

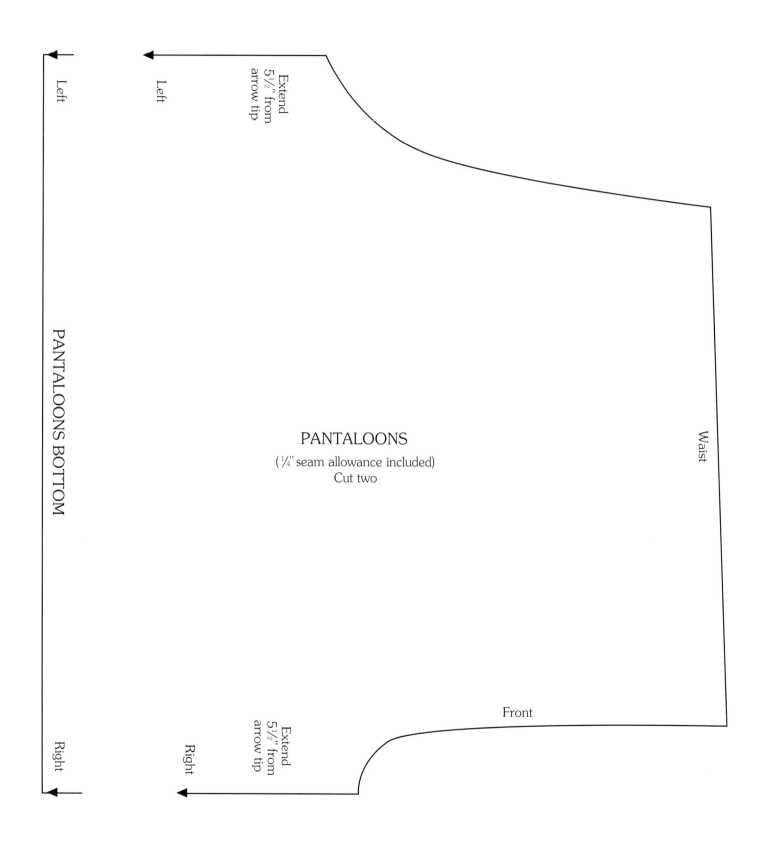

PANTALOONS BOTTOM

Left

Left

Extend
5½" from
arrow tip

PANTALOONS

(¼" seam allowance included)
Cut two

Waist

Front

Extend
5½" from
arrow tip

Right

Right

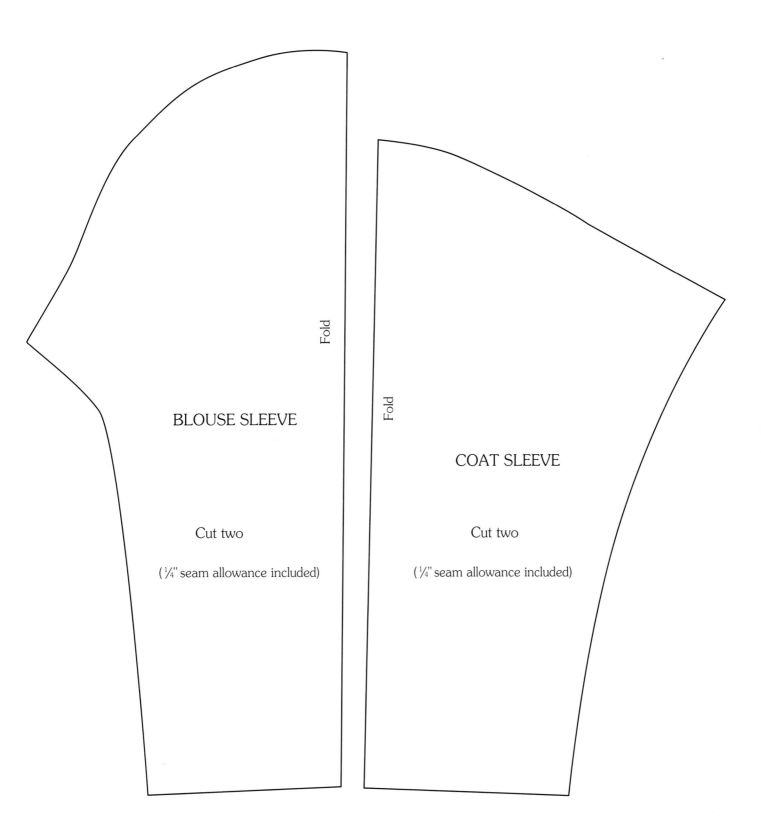

BLOUSE SLEEVE

Cut two

(¼" seam allowance included)

Fold

Fold

COAT SLEEVE

Cut two

(¼" seam allowance included)

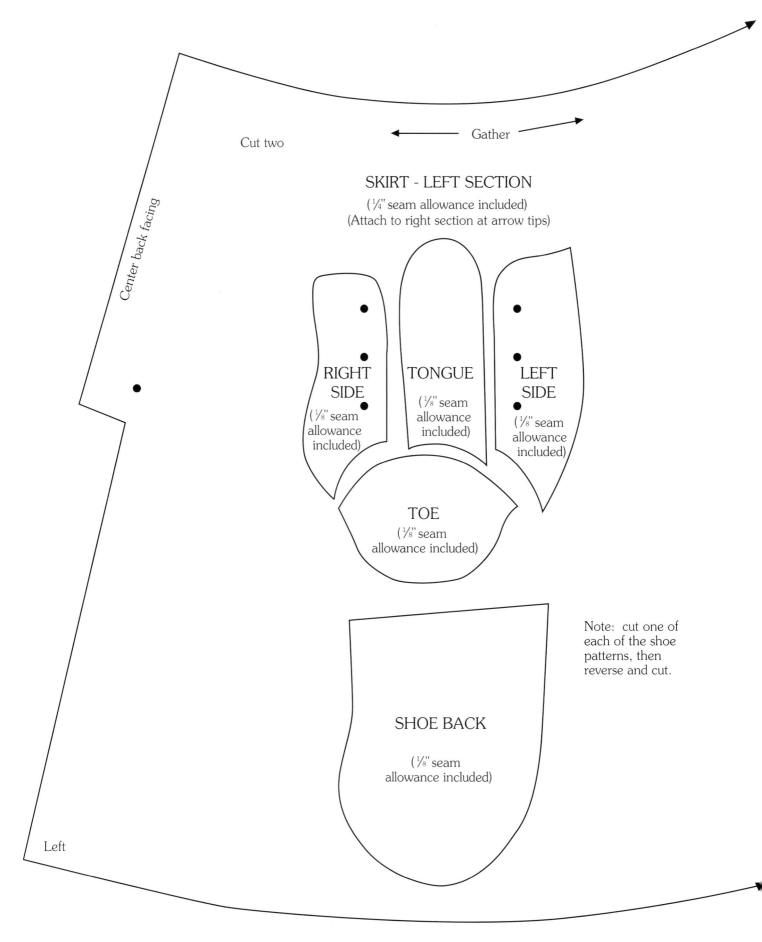

Cut two

Gather

Center back facing

SKIRT - LEFT SECTION
(¼" seam allowance included)
(Attach to right section at arrow tips)

RIGHT
SIDE
(⅛" seam
allowance
included)

TONGUE
(⅛" seam
allowance
included)

LEFT
SIDE
(⅛" seam
allowance
included)

TOE
(⅛" seam
allowance included)

Note: cut one of
each of the shoe
patterns, then
reverse and cut.

SHOE BACK

(⅛" seam
allowance included)

Left

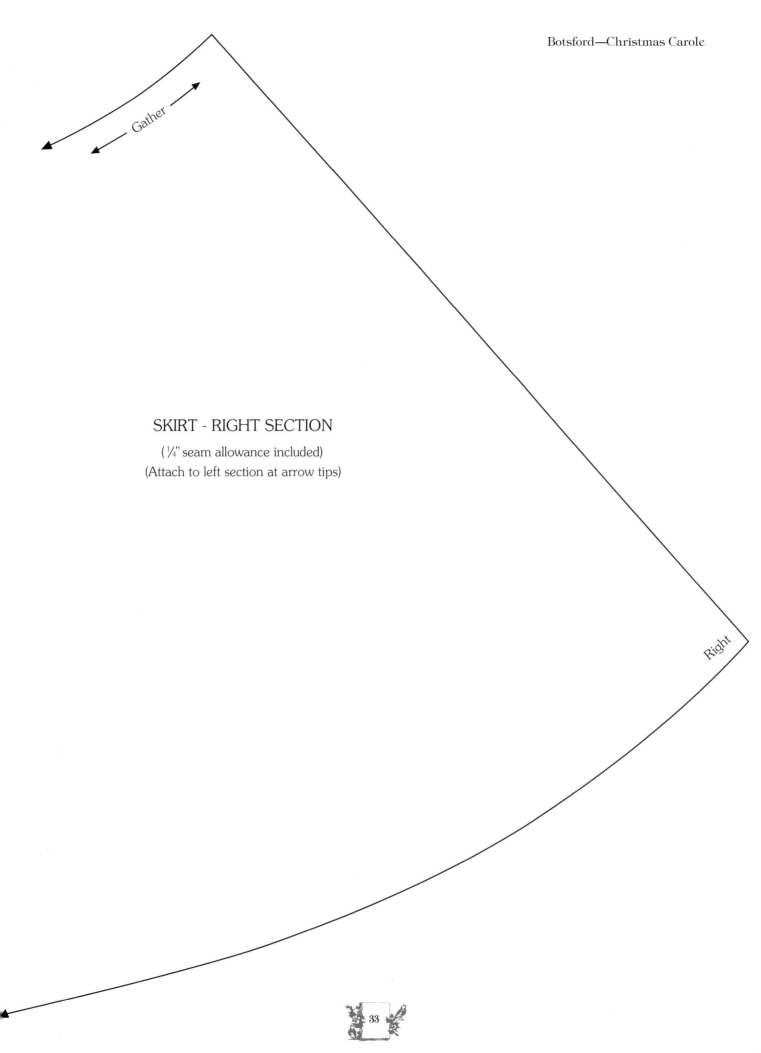

Gather

SKIRT - RIGHT SECTION

($\frac{1}{4}$" seam allowance included)
(Attach to left section at arrow tips)

Right

## Double Nine-Patch Quilt

*Lavender Bags is a group of unbelievably talented quiltmakers who gather monthly. A year ago, they decided it would be fun to make a group quilt top for each member; I surprised them by picking Christmas colors for mine, instead of red, white, and blue. Since the group includes Laura Nownes, co-author with Diana McClun of* Quilts! Quilts!! Quilts!!!, *we decided on the Double Nine-Patch in that book—which I shall always call the Page 34 Quilt. We each made up 24 nine-patches and 24 alternate squares; at the meetings, there was a flurry of sewing, ironing, color arranging. The recipient would bring her large triangles, and the quilt would emerge. In two hours, she would take home a complete top made by her friends. (Each one of us knows that hers is the best!) Thank you Sandy for setting up your wonderful studio each month; and thank you to the loyal stitchers—Dena Canty, Diane Clements, Lynne Hatcher, Claire Jarratt, Barbara Jenkins, Sandy Klop, Karen Matsumoto, Laura Nownes, Kandy Petersen, Rosalee Sanders, and Ethel Selbert. I encourage every reader to form a group and make your own Page 34 Quilts!*

*When I called Laura and Diana for permission to use the Page 34 Quilt in this book, they were, as always, gracious and generous; and Laura immediately volunteered to write the directions for you — doubly appropriate, since she also helped to make this one. I first met Laura when she worked at Diana's shop, and I was immediately drawn to her gentle, sweet charm. I hope you all have a friend like Laura, someone with the gift to make you feel needed, loved, and important. She is an accomplished seamstress, a talented quiltmaker, and the author of a number of books on her own, as well as co-author with Diana of three books, most recently* Quilts, Quilts, and More Quilts!

*Block size is 12¾" square; finished quilt is 73" x 98".*

## Fabric

- **Nine-patch blocks:** ⅛ yard each of 10 light and 10 dark fabrics
- **Alternate blocks:** ⅛ yard each of 12 fabrics
- **Setting triangles:** 2 yards of co-ordinating fabric (#1) and 1¾ yards of another co-ordinating fabric (#2)
- **Border:** 1¼ yards cut on the crosswise grain, or 2 ⅞ yards cut on the lengthwise grain
- **Backing:** 5¾ yards
- **Binding:** ⅝ yard (¼" wide finished)

## Cutting

Cut all strips on the crosswise grain.

- **Nine-patch blocks:** Cut all 20 fabrics into 1½"-wide strips.
- **Alternate blocks:** Cut all 12 fabrics into 3½"-wide strips, then into 3½" squares.
- **Setting triangles**: Cut both fabrics into 8"-wide strips, then into 8" squares. Cut all the squares in half diagonally. You need 68 triangles of fabric #1 and 72 triangles of fabric #2.
- **Border:** Crosswise, cut nine strips 5" x 42"; lengthwise, cut four strips 5" wide by the length of the fabric.
- **Binding:** Cut nine strips 1¾" wide and piece them together.

## Assembly

*Use a ¼" seam allowance throughout.*

1. Arrange six strips into combinations of light and dark, three strips each. Make one set with dark in the middle and one set with light in the middle.
2. Sew the strips into sets. Then cut the sets apart every 1½", as shown.

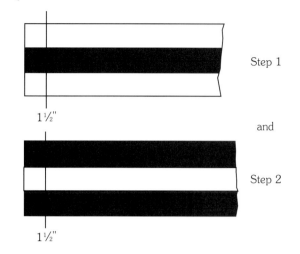

Step 1

and

Step 2

3. Sew the pieces into nine-patch blocks, assembling nine of each combination, as shown.

Step 3

4. Make 166 nine-patch blocks from the remaining 1½" strips in the same way. You will need a total of 175 nine-patch blocks. (The 20 fabrics will make 180 blocks.)
5. Sew the nine-patch and alternate blocks together, as shown. You will need a total of 35 sets.

Step 5

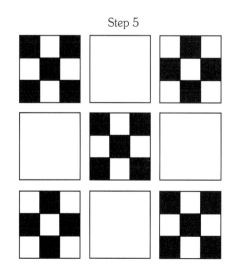

6. Sew the setting triangles to the block sides, as shown. Make 18 of these units with fabric #1 and 17 with fabric #2.

Step 6

7. The setting triangles are cut slightly too large. Trim the excess and straighten the edges. Each unit should measure 13¼" square when finished.
8. Sew the pieced blocks together into a straight setting, alternating setting triangle fabrics. Use the color photograph as a guide.
9. Attach the borders, using your preferred method, to complete the quilt top.

If this is a group project, divide the total number of units (175 nine-patch and 140 alternate blocks) among the participants. The recipient of the quilt top can bring the setting triangles.

♥ Baking has always been an important part of my relationship with Sara and Molly, my daughters. It provides a special time of sharing. The holidays give us an excuse to work and play together in the kitchen. Because there are many young children in our neighborhood, my girls like to make small pumpkin pies for their friends, and they decorate each with shapes (stars, trees, Santas, initials) from extra crust, carefully placed on top before baking. Their friends love the personalized gifts, and the girls enjoy playing Santa's elves, delivering the pies with Daddy.

# Italian Broccoli Casserole
### (Serves 6-8)

2 ten-ounce packages of frozen cut broccoli
2 beaten eggs
1 can of condensed cheddar cheese soup
½ tsp. oregano
1 can of Italian-style stewed tomatoes (14½ ounces)
3 tbsp. grated Parmesan cheese

Cook frozen broccoli in unsalted boiling water for 5-7 minutes. Drain well. Combine eggs, soup, and oregano in a bowl. Stir in tomatoes and broccoli. Pour the mixture into a baking pan and sprinkle with cheese. Bake uncovered at 350° for 30 minutes.

# PAUL PILGRIM

Paul Pilgrim is adored by all who know him. With Gerald Roy he has a pattern company, Pilgrim/Roy; he also owns a wonderful gift shop in San Francisco, he sells fine early American antiques, he is a teacher and lecturer, and he is now designing fabric for P & B Textiles. His knowledge of antiques and the past is legendary; he was among the first to value our ancestor quiltmakers, defending those who made imperfect "quilts of necessity" with the phrase "she did the best she could." Asking him to design a quilt for this book was like being told to eat chocolate daily. I wish you could have him beside you, to talk you through the project: for him, having fun is the first requirement. How I wish I had been his student!

## Oh Holy Night Wall Hanging

*Finished size is 38½" x 46½".*

All measurements given in this project are the size of the pattern piece needed with seam allowance included. **Do not add anything to the measurements listed.**

## Materials Needed

**Stars, flames, candlesticks, and border letters**
- ⅓ yard total of co-ordinating yellow scrap fabrics

**Sky**
- ¾ yard of blue print fabric

**Trees**
- ¼ yard total of co-ordinating green scrap fabrics

**Tree trunks**
- ⅛ yard total of co-ordinating brown scrap fabrics

**Border background**
- ¾ yard of blue print fabric

**Corner blocks and binding**
- ½ yard of green print fabric

**Snow and candles**
- ⅓ yard total of co-ordinating white or light beige print fabrics

**Church walls, roof, windows, door, and tower walls**
- ⅛ yard each of co-ordinating print fabrics

**Optional:**
1 yard of of black yarn (for candlewicks and to separate letters in borders) and approximately 700 multi-colored glass beads (to embellish trees)

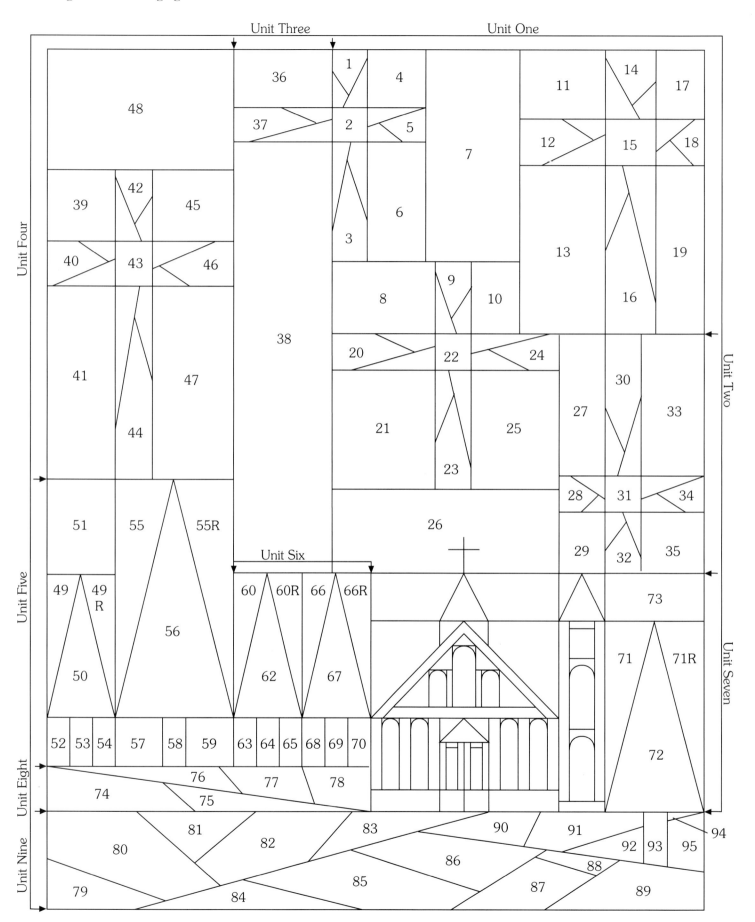

## Pieces Necessary to Make the Wall Hanging

### STAR POINTS

There are no patterns used to make the star points. Follow these instructions to make pieces 1, 3, 5, 9, 12, 14, 16, 18, 20, 23, 24, 28, 30, 32, 34, 37, 40, 42, 44, and 46.

Take the measurement given for each piece, find the center of one narrow end, and cut a diagonal wedge off each side to suit you.

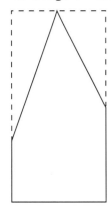

When cutting your diagonal line for the star points, stay at least $\frac{5}{8}$" back from the end of your fabric. This will insure you will not lose your points when you sew the stars together. After you have cut your diagonals, take a scrap piece of your star fabric and sew it to one side of the piece. Press the seam in the easiest direction. Now sew a second piece of star fabric to the other diagonal and press. Using the finished measurement given for each section of the stars, trim the piece to the correct size. This is how I got my stars to all have different points and intersections (refer to the photo of the wall hanging).

### STAR CENTERS

2. 2" x 2"
15. $2\frac{1}{2}$" x $2\frac{1}{2}$"
22. 2" x 2"
31. 2" x 2"
43. 2" x $2\frac{1}{2}$"

### TREES

Trees can be made several ways. You can sew scraps of fabric together and then use templates to cut them out, or you can make each tree out of one piece of fabric.

To make the trees, use templates 50, 56, 62, 67, and 72.

### TREE TRUNKS

53. $1\frac{1}{2}$" x $2\frac{1}{2}$"
58. $1\frac{1}{2}$" x $2\frac{1}{2}$"
64. $1\frac{1}{2}$" x $2\frac{1}{2}$"
69. $1\frac{1}{2}$" x $2\frac{1}{2}$"
93. use template

### SKY

| | |
|---|---|
| 1. 2" x $3\frac{1}{8}$" | 34. 2" x $3\frac{1}{8}$" |
| 3. 2" x $5\frac{5}{8}$" | 35. 3" x 3" |
| 4. 3" x 3" | 36. $4\frac{1}{2}$" x 3" |
| 5. 2" x $3\frac{1}{8}$" | 37. 2" x $4\frac{5}{8}$" |
| 6. 3" x $5\frac{1}{2}$" | 38. $4\frac{1}{2}$" x $18\frac{1}{2}$" |
| 7. $4\frac{1}{2}$" x $9\frac{1}{2}$" | 39. $3\frac{1}{2}$" x $3\frac{1}{2}$" |
| 8. 5" x $3\frac{1}{2}$" | 40. $2\frac{1}{2}$" x $3\frac{5}{8}$" |
| 9. 2" x $3\frac{5}{8}$" | 41. $3\frac{1}{2}$" x $8\frac{1}{2}$" |
| 10. $2\frac{1}{2}$" x $3\frac{1}{2}$" | 42. 2" x $3\frac{5}{8}$" |
| 11. $4\frac{1}{2}$" x $3\frac{1}{2}$" | 44. 2" x $8\frac{5}{8}$" |
| 12. $4\frac{5}{8}$" x $2\frac{1}{2}$" | 45. 4" x $3\frac{1}{2}$" |
| 13. $4\frac{1}{2}$" x $7\frac{1}{2}$" | 46. $2\frac{1}{2}$" x $4\frac{1}{8}$" |
| 14. $2\frac{1}{2}$" x $3\frac{5}{8}$" | 47. 4" x $8\frac{1}{2}$" |
| 16. $2\frac{1}{2}$" x $7\frac{5}{8}$" | 48. $8\frac{1}{2}$" x $5\frac{1}{2}$" |
| 17. $2\frac{1}{2}$" x $3\frac{1}{2}$" | 49. & 49R. use template |
| 18. $2\frac{1}{2}$" x $2\frac{5}{8}$" | 51. $3\frac{1}{2}$" x $4\frac{1}{2}$" |
| 19. $2\frac{1}{2}$" x $7\frac{1}{2}$" | 52 & 54.  $1\frac{1}{2}$" x $2\frac{1}{2}$" |
| 20. 2" x $5\frac{1}{8}$" | 55 & 55R. use template |
| 21. 5" x $5\frac{1}{2}$" | 57 & 59.  $2\frac{1}{2}$" x $2\frac{1}{2}$" |
| 23. 2" x $5\frac{5}{8}$" | 60 & 60R. use template |
| 24. 2" x $4\frac{5}{8}$" | 63 & 65. $1\frac{1}{2}$" x $2\frac{1}{2}$" |
| 25. $4\frac{1}{2}$" x $5\frac{1}{2}$" | 66 & 66R. use template |
| 26. $10\frac{1}{2}$" x 4" | 68 & 70. $1\frac{1}{2}$" x $2\frac{1}{2}$" |
| 27. $2\frac{1}{2}$" x $6\frac{1}{2}$" | 71 & 71R. use template |
| 28. 2" x $2\frac{5}{8}$" | 73. $4\frac{1}{2}$" x $2\frac{1}{2}$" |
| 29. $2\frac{1}{2}$" x 3" | 96 & 96R. use template |
| 30. 2" x $6\frac{5}{8}$" | 99. $1\frac{1}{2}$" x $1\frac{3}{4}$" |
| 32. 2" x $3\frac{1}{8}$" | 105 & 105R. use template |
| 33. 3" x $6\frac{1}{2}$" | 107 & 107R. use template |

### CHURCH

#### Roof

97. use template
106. use template
116. use template
117. use template
125. use template

#### Tower Walls and Church Sections

98. $1\frac{1}{2}$" x $\frac{3}{4}$"
102 & 103. 1" x 8"
104. $2\frac{1}{2}$" x 1"
115. use template
123. $3\frac{1}{2}$" x $1\frac{1}{2}$", cut 2

## Walls

108 & 108R. use template
110. ¾" x 2", cut 2
111 & 111R. use template
113. use template
114 & 114R. use template
118. 1" x 3½", cut 2
120. 1" x 3½", cut 2
122. 1" x 3½", cut 2
124 & 124R. use template

## Door

126. 1" x ¾", cut 2
128. ¾" x 2½", cut 2
129. ¾" x 2½", cut 2
130. 1½" x 1½", cut 2

## Stained Glass Windows

The window templates have the seam allowances included on three sides. They do not have the seam allowances on the arch. When you trace the templates on the back of your fabric, trace the arch line, then add extra fabric above the arch when you cut out the windows. You will need approximately ¼" extra to turn under to appliqué the windows to the wall fabric that fills in the arch above the window.

- 100 & 101. use templates.
  Cut wall fabric 1½" x 1½". After you have cut out the windows, turn under fabric at arch line and appliqué curve to wall fabric ½" from top.
- 109. use template, cut 2
  Cut wall fabric for these windows 1¼" x ¾". Appliqué curve ¼" from top.
- 112. use template
  Cut wall fabric for this window 1½" x 1". Appliqué curve ¼" from top.
- 119 & 121. use template, cut 4
  Cut wall fabrics for these windows 1¼" x 1". Appliqué curves ¼" from top.
- 127. 1" x 2¼", cut 2

## SNOW

This area is made up of the following templates: 74, 75, 76, 77, 78, 79, 80, 81, 82, 83, 84, 85, 86, 87, 88, 89, 90, 91, 92, 94, & 95. Use as many different snow colors as you wish. There is no set pattern to placement of colors.

## Sewing Instructions

### UNIT ONE

1. Lay out pieces 1–19 to form this section.
2. First we are going to sew the star points on pieces 1, 3, 5, 9, 12, 14, 16, and 18. Look back to the instructions in the beginning of the project to refresh yourself on how to put on the points.

Here are the exact sizes you will trim each piece to after you have sewn on the scrap pieces for the points. Make sure your pieces are cut to these sizes or they will not sew into place.

1. 2" x 3"
3. 2 x 5½"
5. 2" x 3"
9. 2" x 3½"
12. 2½" x 4½"
14. 2½" x 3½"
16. 2½" x 7½"
18. 2½" x 2½"

As you finish each one of these sections, set it back in place.

3. Sew pieces 1, 2, & 3 together. Press under 2. Set back in place.
4. Sew 4, 5, & 6 together. Press away from 5.
5. Sew step 3 and step 4 units together.
6. Sew 7 to the side of step 5 unit. Set back in place.
7. Sew 8, 9, & 10 together.
8. Sew Step 7 unit to the bottom of step 6 unit. Set back in place.
9. Sew 11, 12, & 13 together. Press away from 12. Set back in place.
10. Sew 14, 15, & 16 together. Press under 15. Set back in place.
11. Sew 17, 18, & 19 together. Press away from 18. Set back in place.
12. Sew step 9 unit to left of step 10 unit.
13. Sew step 11 unit to the right of step 12 unit.
14. Sew step 13 unit to the right of step 8 unit.
   **This is now Unit One.** Set it back in place.

### UNIT TWO

1. Lay out pieces 20–35. Sew star points on pieces 20, 23, 24, 28, 30, 32, & 34. Trim to the following sizes:

20. 2" x 5"
23. 2" x 5½"
24. 2" x 4½"
28. 2" x 2½"
30. 2" x 6½"
32. 2" x 3"
34. 2" x 3"

Set these pieces back in place.

2. Sew 20 & 21 together. Press under 21. Set back in place.
3. Sew 22 & 23 together. Press under 22. Set back in place.
4. Sew 24 & 25 together. Press under 25. Set back in place
5. Sew step units 2, 3, & 4 together.
6. Sew 26 to the bottom of step 5 unit. Set back in place.
7. Sew 27, 28, & 29 together. Press away from 28. Set back in place.
8. Sew 30, 31, & 32 together. Press under 31. Set back in place.
9. Sew 33, 34, & 35 together. Press away from 34. Set back in place.
10. Sew step 7 unit to step 8 unit.
11. Sew step 9 unit to the right of step 10 unit.
12. Sew step 6 unit to the left of step 11 unit. **This is now Unit Two.** Set it back in place.

## UNIT THREE

1. Lay out pieces 36–38 to form this section. Sew star points to piece 37 to make it complete. Trim to 4½" x 2".
2. Sew 36, 37, & 38 together. Press away from 37. **This is now Unit Three.** Set it back in place.

## UNIT FOUR

1. Lay out pieces 39–48 to form this section. Sew star points on pieces 40, 42, 44, & 46. Trim to the following sizes:
   40. 2½" x 3½"
   42. 2" x 3½"
   44. 2" x 8½"
   46. 2½" x 4"

2. Sew 39, 40, & 41 together. Press away from 40. Set back in place.
3. Sew 42, 43, & 44 together. Press under 43. Set back in place.

4. Sew 45, 46, & 47 together. Press away from 46. Set back in place.
5. Sew step 2 & 3 units together.
6. Sew step 4 unit to the right of step 5 unit.
7. Sew 48 across the top of step 6 unit. **This is now Unit Four.** Set it back in place.

## UNIT FIVE

1. Lay out pieces 49–59 to form this section. Sew 49 & 49R to the sides of 50. Set back in place.
2. Sew 52, 53, & 54 together. Press under 53.
3. Sew step 2 unit to the bottom of step 1 unit.
4. Sew 51 to the top of step 3 unit. Set back in place.
5. Sew 55, & 55R to the sides of 56. Set back in place.
6. Sew 57, 58, & 59 together. Press under 58.
7. Sew step 6 unit to the bottom of step 5 unit.
8. Sew step 4 and step 7 units together. **This is now Unit Five.** Set it back in place.

## UNIT SIX

1. Lay out pieces 60–70 to form this section. Sew 60 & 60R to the sides of 62. Set back in place.
2. Sew 63, 64, & 65 together. Press under 64.
3. Sew step 2 unit to the bottom of step 1 unit. Set back in place.
4. Sew 66 & 66R to the sides of 67. Set back in place.
5. Sew 68, 69, & 70 together. Press under 69.
6. Sew step 5 unit to the bottom of step 4 unit.
7. Sew step 3 and step 6 units together. **This is now Unit Six.** Set it back in place.

## UNIT SEVEN

1. Lay out pieces 71–73 to form this section. Sew 71 & 71R to the sides of 72.
2. Sew 73 across the top of step 1 unit. **This is now Unit Seven.** Set it back in place.

## UNIT EIGHT

1. Lay out pieces 74–78 to form this section. Sew 74, & 75 together. Set back in place.
2. Sew 76, 77, & 78 together. Be careful when pressing these pieces. They will distort.

3. Sew step 1 and 2 units together. **This is now Unit Eight.** Set it back in place.

## UNIT NINE

1. Lay out pieces 79–94 to form this section. Sew 79 & 80 together. Set back in place.
2. Sew 81, 82, & 83 together.
3. Sew step 1 & 2 units together. Set back in place.
4. Sew 84, 85, & 86 together. Set back in place.
5. Sew 87 & 88 together.
6. Sew 89 to the side of step 5 unit.
7. Sew step 4 & 6 units together. Set back in place.
8. Sew 90, 91, & 92 together.
9. Sew 93 to the side of step 8 unit. Set back in place.
10. Sew 94 & 95 together.
11. Sew step 10 unit to the side of step 9 unit.
12. Sew step 7 & 11 units together.
13. Sew step 3 unit to step 12 unit. **This is now Unit Nine.** Set it back in place.

## CHURCH SEWING INSTRUCTIONS

Lay out pieces 96–130 to form this section. Here are the window sizes you should trim your pieces to match. The windows with the wall background will form rectangles.

100. $1\frac{1}{2}$" x $3\frac{1}{2}$"
101. $1\frac{1}{2}$" x $3\frac{1}{2}$"
109. $1\frac{1}{4}$" x 2" cut 2
112. $1\frac{1}{2}$" x 3"
119. $1\frac{1}{4}$" x $3\frac{1}{2}$", cut 2
121. $1\frac{1}{4}$" x $3\frac{1}{2}$", cut 2

1. Sew 96 & 96R to the sides of 97. Set back in place.
2. Sew 98 & 99 together. Press under 99.
3. Sew 100 to the bottom of step 2 unit.
4. Sew 101 to the bottom of step 3 unit.
5. Sew 102 & 103 to the sides of step 4 unit. Press under step 4 unit.
6. Sew 104 to the bottom of step 5 unit.
7. Sew step 1 & 6 units together. Set back in place.
8. Sew 105 & 105R to the side of 106. Set back in place.

9. Sew 107 & 108 together. Press under 107. Set back in place.
10. Sew 107R & 108R together. Press under 107R. Set back in place.
11. Sew 109 & 110 together. Check drawing to make sure 110 is on the correct side. Press under 109. Make two units.
12. Sew 111 to the top of the step 11 unit.
13. Sew one step 12 unit to each side of 112.
14. Sew 113 to the top of the step 13 unit.
15. Sew 114 & 114R to the sides of the step 14 unit.
16. Sew 115 across the bottom of step 15 unit.
17. Sew 116 to the right side of the step 16 unit.
18. Sew 117 to the left side of the step 17 unit.
19. Sew step 9 unit to the left and step 10 unit to the right side of step 18 unit. Set back in place.
20. Sew 118, 119, 120, 121, & 122 together. Press under 119 & 121. Make two units.
21. Sew 123 across the bottom of the two step 20 units. Set back in place.
22. Sew 124 & 124R to the sides of 125. Set back in place.
23. Sew 126 & 127 together. Press under 127. Make two.
24. Sew 128 & 129 to the sides of the two step 23 units.
25. Sew 130 across the bottom of the step 24 units.
26. Sew the two step 25 units together.
27. Sew step 26 unit to the bottom of step 22 unit.
28. Sew one step 21 unit to each side of step 27 unit. Set back in place.
29. Sew step 8 unit to the top of step 19 unit.
30. Sew step 28 unit to the bottom of step 29 unit.
31. Sew step 7 unit to the right side of step 30 unit to complete the church block.

## ASSEMBLING THE UNITS AND THE CHURCH

1. Sew Unit One to the top of Unit Two.
2. Sew Unit Three to the left side of step 1 unit. Set back in place.
3. Sew Unit Four to the top of Unit Five. Set back in place.

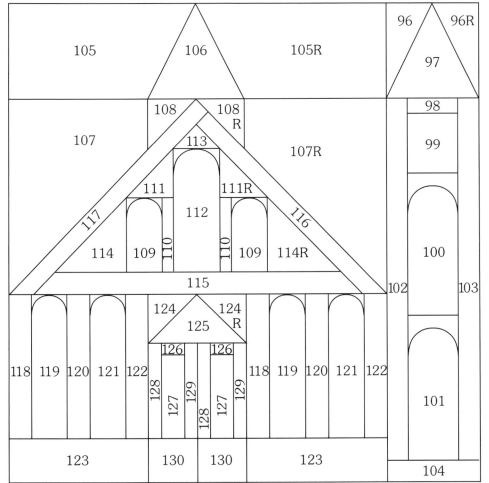

11 & 13. 1" x 1½"
(background fabric)
12. 4½" x 1½"
1, 1R, 2, 9, 9R, & 10.
use templates

## Assembly

1. Lay out pieces to
form candlestick.
2. Sew 1 and 1R to
sides of 2.
3. Sew 3 across the top
of step 2 unit.
4. Sew 4 & 5 to sides of
step 3 unit. Set back
in place.
5. Sew 6, 7, & 8 to-
gether. Set back in
place.
6. Sew 9 and 9R to
sides of 10. Set back
in place.
7. Sew 11, 12, & 13
together. Set back in
place.
8. Sew step 4 unit to the
top of step 5 unit.

4. Sew Unit Seven to the right side of the
church. Set back in place.
5. Beginning at the right side, sew Unit Eight to
the bottom of Unit Six. Stop short at tree
trunk #64.
6. Sew step 5 unit to the left side of the church.
7. Sew step 2 unit across the top of step 6 unit.
8. Sew step 3 unit to the left side of step 7 unit.
9. Now continue sewing Unit Eight across the
bottom of step 8 unit.
10. Sew Unit Nine across the bottom of step 9
unit to complete the center of the Wall Hanging. Center should measure 28½" x 36½"
(including seam allowance).

## CANDLESTICK
### Pieces To Cut
3. 3½" x ¾"
4 & 5. 1½" x 1½" (background fabric)
6 & 8. 2½" x 2½" (background fabric)
7. 1½" x 2½"

9. Sew step 6 unit to the bottom of step 8 unit.
10. Sew step 7 unit to the bottom of step 9 unit
to complete the candlestick.

You need two of these candlesticks, one for
each side border.

## CANDLE SEWING INSTRUCTIONS
### Pieces To Cut
14. 1⅞" square, then cut diagonally
(background fabric)
15. 1½" x 13⅞", cut 45° at one end,
cut 2. Check photo for direction of 45°.
16 & 17. 2½" x 13½", cut 4 total
(background fabric)

## Assembly
1. Sew 14 to the top of 15.
2. Sew 16 to the left side of step 1 unit.
3. Sew 17 to the right side of step 2 unit.

You will need two candles, one for each side border. Check direction; candle should have 45° angle.

## FLAME SEWING INSTRUCTIONS

Using template, cut one piece from each. Now reverse all templates and cut another set. You now have enough pieces to make the two flame units, one for each side.

1. Sew 18 & 19 together.
2. Sew 20 to the bottom of step 1 unit.
3. Sew 21 across the bottom of step 2 unit.
4. Sew 22 to the right side of step 3 unit.

You need to make two flame units. They must face opposite directions.

Flame piece #18 can be made from one color fabric, or sewn from strip scraps of fabric as I have done.

19, 20, 21, & 22 are all background fabric.

## LETTER SEWING INSTRUCTIONS

You have the option of adding yarn between the letters to help define them if the scrap fabrics you are using are too close in color. To determine the amount of yarn to cut, measure each section where the letters meet, adding $\frac{1}{2}$" extra so the ends can be sewn into the seam allowances. Use white glue to keep the ends from fraying. Using a single strand of co-ordinated quilting thread, tack down the yarn (the laid thread) with small stitches at regular intervals (called "couching").

## LETTER O SEWING INSTRUCTIONS

### Pieces To Cut

24 & 26. $1\frac{1}{2}$" x $2\frac{1}{2}$"
25. $2\frac{1}{2}$" x $2\frac{1}{2}$" (background fabric)
27 & 28. $4\frac{1}{2}$" x $1\frac{1}{2}$"

### Assembly

1. Sew 24, 25, & 26 together.
2. Sew 27 to the top and 28 to the bottom of step 1 unit. You will need to make 2 O's.

## LETTERS H AND I SEWING INSTRUCTIONS

### Pieces To Cut

29 & 31. $2\frac{1}{2}$" x 2" (background fabric)
30. $2\frac{1}{2}$" x $1\frac{1}{2}$"
32 & 33. $1\frac{1}{2}$" x $4\frac{1}{2}$"

### Assembly

1. Sew 29, 30, & 31 together.
2. Sew 32 to the left and 33 to the right of step 1 unit. You need four of these units (3 H's, and 1 H turned on its side for an I).

## LETTERS L AND Y SEWING INSTRUCTIONS

### Pieces To Cut

35. $3\frac{1}{2}$" x $1\frac{1}{2}$"
36. $1\frac{1}{2}$" x $4\frac{1}{2}$"
41. $1\frac{1}{2}$" x 2"
42. 2" x 2" (background fabric)
34, 37, 38, 39, & 40. use templates

### Assembly

1. Sew 34 and 35 together.
2. Sew 36 to the left side of step 1 unit. Set back in place.
3. Sew 37 and 38 together. Set back in place.
4 Sew 39 and 40 together. Set back in place.
5. Sew 41 and 42 together.
6. Sew step 5 unit to the bottom of step 4 unit. Set back in place.
7. Using Y-seam construction, sew step 2 unit to step 3 unit. Start at the top and stop sewing $\frac{1}{4}$" from the bottom.
8. Sew step 6 unit to step 7 unit, using Y-seam construction. Start at the top and stop sewing at seam line of Y-intersection.
9. Adjust unsewn intersection as needed, then begin sewing at the top of the Y-intersection, and sew down to base of the Y to complete the block. Make sure you do not catch any of the intersection top seam in the base seam. Press the base seam open, and press the other two top seams down toward it. This will give you a perfect intersection at the Y.

## LETTER N SEWING INSTRUCTIONS
### Pieces To Cut
46 & 47. 1½" x 4½"
43, 44 & 45. use templates

### Assembly
1. Sew 43 to the top of 44.
2. Sew 45 to the bottom of step 1 unit.
3. Sew 46 to the left and 47 to the right of step 2 unit.

## LETTER G SEWING INSTRUCTIONS
### Pieces To Cut
48. 1½" x 1" (background fabric)
49. 1½" x 1"
50. 2½" x 1" (background fabric)
51. 2 ½" x 1½"
52. 1½" x 2½" (background fabric)
53 & 54. 3½" x 1½"
55. 1½" x 4½"

### Assembly
1. Sew 48 and 49 together. Set back in place.
2. Sew 50 and 51 together.
3. Sew step 1 unit to the bottom of step 2 unit.
4. Sew 52 to the left side of step 3 unit.
5. Sew 53 to the top and 54 to the bottom of step 4 unit.
6. Sew 55 to the left side of step 5 unit.

## LETTER T SEWING INSTRUCTIONS
### Pieces To Cut
56 & 58. 2" x 3½" (background fabric)
57. 1½" x 3½"
59. 4½" x 1½"

### Assembly
1. Sew 56, 57, & 58 together.
2. Sew 59 across the top of step 1 unit.

## OH HOLY BORDER ASSEMBLY
### Pieces To Cut
60 & 62. 1¼" x 4½" (background fabric)
61. 4½" x 4½" (background fabric)
63 & 64. 28 ½" x 1" (background fabric)

### Assembly
1. Sew 60 to the left of the O.
2. Sew the H to the right side of step 1 unit.
3. Sew 61 to the right side of step 2 unit. Set back in place.
4. Sew H, O, L, & Y units together.
5. Sew 62 to the right side of step 4 unit.
6. Sew step 3 unit to step 5 unit.
7. Sew 63 to the top and 64 to the bottom of step 6 unit.

Completed border should now measure 28½" x 5½" (including seam allowance).

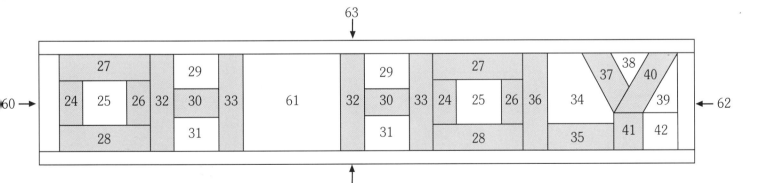

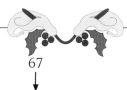

67

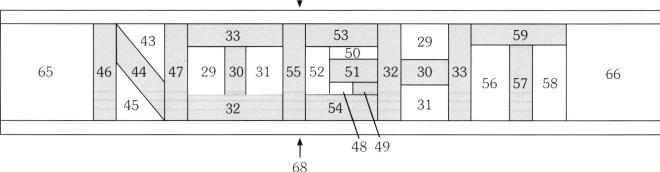

| 65 | 46 | 43 / 44 / 45 | 47 | 29 | 30 | 31 | 55 | 52 | 53 / 50 / 51 / 54 | 32 | 29 / 30 / 31 | 33 | 59 / 56 / 57 / 58 | 66 |

48  49

68

## NIGHT BORDER ASSEMBLY
### Pieces To Cut
65 & 66.  $4\frac{1}{2}$" x $4\frac{1}{2}$" (background fabric)
67 & 68.  $28\frac{1}{2}$" x 1" (background fabric)

### Assembly
1. Sew N, I, G, H, & T together.
2. Sew 65 to the left and 66 to the right of step 1 unit.
3. Sew 67 to the top and 68 to the bottom of step 2 unit.
Completed border should now measure $28\frac{1}{2}$" x $5\frac{1}{2}$" (including seam allowance).

## SIDE BORDER ASSEMBLY
23.  $5\frac{1}{2}$" x $13\frac{1}{2}$" (background fabric)
1. Lay out pieces to make the border: Candle-stick unit, Candle unit, Flame unit, and #23. Make sure the candle faces properly to match the direction of the flame.
2. Sew all four sections together to complete the side borders.
Completed borders should measure $5\frac{1}{2}$" x $36\frac{1}{2}$" (including seam allowance). If you prefer, cut two 4" lengths of yarn for the candle wicks. Insert one end of yarn into fabric front 1" above bottom of flame, leaving a 1" tail at the fabric back. Insert other end into top of candle, so the wick forms a straight vertical line, and leaving a 1" tail at the fabric back. Secure tails and couch the wick with co-ordinating quilting thread.

## BORDER SEWING INSTRUCTIONS
Corner Blocks $5\frac{1}{2}$" x $5\frac{1}{2}$", cut 4
1. Sew Oh Holy border to the top of the wall hanging.
2. Sew Night border to the bottom of the wall hanging.
3. Sew one corner block to each end of the side borders.
4. Sew one border to each side of the quilt to complete the Oh Holy Night wall hanging. Check the photograph for correct position of the candles. If you prefer, add multi-colored beads to trees.
Completed top should measure $38\frac{1}{2}$" x $46\frac{1}{2}$" (including seam allowance).

## Backing
Backing should be 42" x 50". It can be a pieced back or a one-piece back. The back on my wall hanging is pieced from three strips of fabric from top to bottom. The center strip is the narrowest. The two outside strips are equal in width.

## Batting
I use Heirloom® Cotton Batting. It gives a wonderful flat wall hanging and quilts very well.

## Binding
I cut my binding on the straight of the grain. I cut my strip $2\frac{1}{4}$" wide, then press it in half to make a strip $1\frac{1}{8}$" wide. I set my machine for a $\frac{1}{4}$" seam, matching the raw edges, and apply the binding to the front of the quilt. I then bring the binding around to the back and finish by hand.
Finish the wall hanging using your preferred methods.

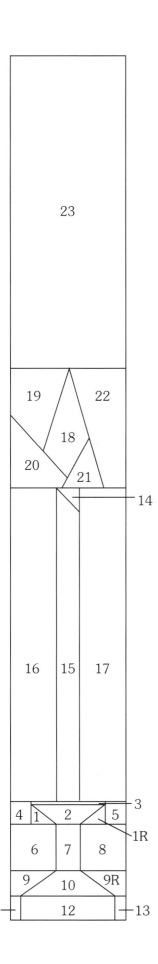

❤ The Pilgrim Christmas Tradition grew out of something my mother and father did for me when I was a small child. Every December, after our tree was put up, all the presents from aunts, uncles, grandparents, cousins, and friends were arranged under the tree on top of the glittered cotton snow that hid the tree stand. They were arranged so everyone had a place of honor. On Christmas Eve, after making the rounds to visit all the family, my mother, father, and I would come home, light the fireplace, and sit near the tree, opening our gifts.

When the last package was opened, it was time for bed. My bedroom was in the back wing of the house, and I was usually so tired that I never heard what took place after I went to bed. But, on Christmas morning when I woke there would be a special gift from Santa. It was understood that Santa brought only one gift and that all the other gifts that were opened the night before were from family and friends. I never could figure out how Santa knew exactly what I wanted.

As I grew older and realized that Santa was a wonderful friend that I had loved for at least ten years, he was about to be replaced by reality and I would not experience the excitement of looking forward to what Santa had brought while I was asleep. This was cause for a family meeting. Mom, Dad, and I sat down to see what we could do to keep this tradition alive. It was decided that each of us would save our best gift for each other till Christmas morning. I continued to receive my special gift on Christmas morning, and it always had a card that read "From Santa."

This Pilgrim Christmas Tradition was shared by the three of us until I lost my mother in 1986. My father and I kept the tradition until I lost him three years later. I now keep the tradition alive with friends that have taken the place of family. Funny how this simple tradition, now shared with friends, allows me to remember my parents with love and to thank them for giving me such a special and wonderful life. I will always miss them, but every Christmas I thank them for having started the Pilgrim Christmas Tradition.

## Christmas Breakfast

Waffles were only served on Christmas morning in the Pilgrim home. Not that they were difficult to make, they were difficult to cook. That old waffle iron was the electric appliance from Hell. The first ones always stuck. If they did not stick, there was always too much batter in the thing and it oozed out down the side of the iron and onto the sink, where it stuck in the tile grout.

The waffles of choice for Christmas morning were Walnut Bacon Waffles. Always served with Grandmother Pilgrim's strawberry preserves, homemade apple butter, or maple syrup.

# Walnut-Bacon Waffles

**Sift together**
1¾ cups of sifted cake flour
2 tsp. double-acting baking powder
½ tsp. salt
1 tbsp. sugar

**Beat well**
3 egg yolks.
Add 2 to 7 tbsp. melted butter (depending
 on how much your waffle iron sticks) and
1½ cups of milk.
Fold in ¾ cup of chopped walnuts.

Make a well in the sifted ingredients and pour in the liquids. Combine with a few quick strokes. The result will resemble muffin batter. Add the walnuts.

**Beat until stiff but not dry**
3 egg whites.
Fold them into the batter until
 barely blended.

**Cut in half**
6 to 12 slices of bacon.

When the waffle iron is hot, open the lid and pour in enough batter to cover about ⅔ of the surface. After it spreads, lay 2 half-strips of bacon on top of each section of the waffle iron. Close the lid and wait about 4 minutes, or until steam no longer exits the opening. If the lid does not lift easily, wait about a minute longer.

Serve these waffles with syrup, stewed fruit, honey, or your personal favorite.

This breakfast was accompanied by orange juice and coffee. The one day a year (at home) that I was allowed to have coffee. It was always full of milk and sugar.

The flavor of the bacon and walnuts is one you never forget. This is a breakfast to remember.

Happy eating and a Very Merry Christmas.

# THE CHRISTMAS PROJECTS

Yvonne Porcella: *Jewel-Tone Silk Christmas Vest*

Nicki Becker:
*Folk Art Santa Stocking*

Jean Wells: *Christmas Mini-Socks and Tree Skirt*

Molly Milligan-Cokeley: *Father Christmas* (front)

Molly Milligan-Cokeley: *Father Christmas* (back)

◀ Diana McClun:
*Christmas Table Setting*

Rose Sheifer: *Holiday Letter*

Paul Pilgrim: *Oh Holy Night Wall Hanging*
Quilted by Toni Fisher, Belton, Missouri.

Gerry Kimmel: *Trees Around the World*

Shirley Botsford: *Christmas Carole*

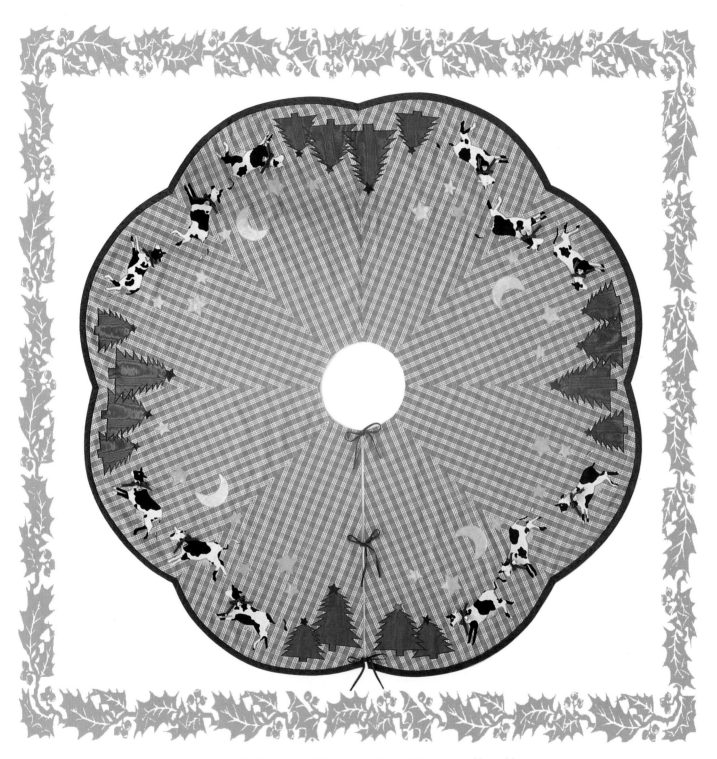

Cathie I. Hoover: *Whimsical Cow Christmas Tree Skirt*

Margaret Peters: *Treetop Angel* (front)

Margaret Peters: *Treetop Angel* (back)

Baby's First
Christmas
1994

With Love
to Aunt Jane
Merry
Christmas

Silent Night
Holy Night
All is calm
all is bright

Margaret Peters: *Angel Ornament*

Lavender Bags: *Double Nine-Patch Quilt*

# DIANA McCLUN

## Christmas Table Setting

Where do I even begin talking about Diana McClun? I have known her since the days when I would visit her shop, Empty Spools. She changed my entire life: when Diana tells you to do something, you don't question or hesitate and so, when she wanted me to tell her customers about my experiences decorating a Christmas tree for the Smithsonian and the White House visits, I thought she was crazy but I did it — and thus began my speaking career. She is the co-author, with Laura Nownes, of some of the best-selling quilt-making books in the world. She also runs the Empty Spools Seminar each year at Asilomar, on the Pacific near Carmel and Monterey.

In addition to all of Diana's many other talents, she is one of the best party-givers I know. I will never forget her daughter Tric's wedding reception: fruit, cheese, and breads spilling out of a pyramid of baskets in the center of the food table, white ceramic geese wearing scarves and peeking from behind the bushes and trees, and quilts spread on the ground for some of the seating. (Diana believes strongly that quilts are to be used, as you can see again in the table setting.)

To decorate my dining area for you, Diana arrived armed with nothing more than a frayed old quilt. (Confession time: she later sent my husband Pete to borrow Tric's chairs, which she felt went better with the setting than my chairs.) She then went to work with what I already owned, selecting from my Santa collection to set the theme, arranging them on the hutch and table, including a Santa at each place for the guest to take home and start another collection. (My Santa collection has inspired Diana's daughter Katie to start her own.) What she did in a short time at my house demonstrates her philosophy that your table decorating doesn't have to be costly or elaborate: start with what you own and love. Any collection can serve not only as decoration; it will also make for great conversation. If you collect bottles, group them on the table with a flower or two in each. I once gave a luncheon and had no flowers, so I stacked eggs on a scale and stuck parsley wherever it fit. And don't get too trapped into any rules. I went to a New Year's Eve party on March first, given by a hostess whose year had started badly: she decided we should all start the year over! So stay loose, and have fun.

♥ Ice cream snowballs have been a dessert tradition for our Christmas eve celebration for as long as I can remember. This Christmas occasion, with lighted birthday candles in front of you, gives you a moment to reflect upon the special essence that is Christmas. The candle represents the light of Jesus; it is a reminder of the unique circumstances of His birth and of His special role in our lives.

# Christmas Snowball

1 gallon of ice cream, vanilla or any favorite flavor
1 package of shredded coconut
12 birthday candles
Holly leaves

Form the ice cream into twelve balls with an ice cream scoop. Roll them gently in a bowl of coconut, covering them. Insert a candle into the center of each ball, place them in a covered dish, and return them to the freezer until serving time. Garnish them with holly leaves.

# YVONNE PORCELLA

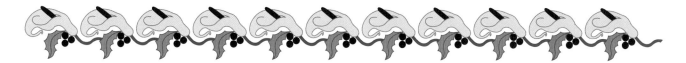

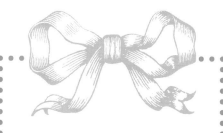

*Yvonne Porcella is the perfect professional in every way. She is a renowned quiltmaker, the author and publisher of several books, a motivating force behind the promotion of respect for art quilts among art museums worldwide, involved in all aspects of our business but with always enough time to take on another project — like this one for me. She has long been my role model in this business, for both her business sense and her generous personality. (I don't pretend to emulate her as an artist!) I shouldn't have been surprised that she was so willing to help us out with this stunning vest: she's in the midst of only a few dozen major projects at the moment (including writing another book).*

## Jewel-Tone Silk Christmas Vest

**V**ests are a wonderful fashion accessory; a vest can be made in a single day, a vest takes a scant amount of fabric, and you can have at least a dozen in your wardrobe. You can make vests for each season or each month, and they are a great way to try new patchwork or strip-piecing designs. For this Christmas vest, I have used the basic vest pattern that is featured in my book *Pieced Clothing VARIATIONS* (available from C&T Publishing). I altered the front of this vest by adding a dipped shape to the center front. You can also use another commercial vest pattern, or your own design. I do recommend that you use a pattern that has flat shapes: shaping darts or curved side seams distort the patchwork if you follow my directions for flat strip-piecing.

Through the years I have collected remnants of Indian and Thai silks in jewel tones. For this vest you do not need a large amount of one particular color, except for the lining. This sample vest is a size 12 medium and required only five-eighths of a yard of 45"-wide fabric for the inside. If you use patchwork, you may need more fabric, depending upon the design. I used eight colors of silks and added one piece of silver fabric. My color scheme began with a beautiful plaid silk; I added solids to compliment the plaid. This vest could also be made with jewel-color cottons.

The patchwork design is based on the traditional Log Cabin block. I cut the center square in half diagonally and used the triangle as the beginning of the block, surrounding it with the solids. Alternating the placement of the bars creates an off-center block: in order to see the process, follow the placement of the bars.

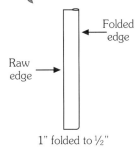

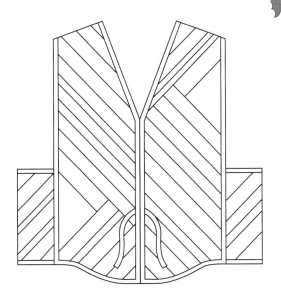

Log Cabin piecing with folded fabric overlay added in some seams. The overlay provides a narrow strip of contrasting color without your having to piece a narrow strip of silk.

## Fabric Requirements

All silk fabrics are 36"-40" wide.

**Plaid:** ¼ yard. Cut a 4½" square, and pieced bias strips 1½" x 72".

**Chartreuse, rose tweed, silver, & turquoise:** Cut two strips each, 1½" x 40".

**Purple:** Cut one strip 1½" x 40", one strip 3" x 40", and one strip 1" x 40".

**Ruby red & orange:** Cut one strip each 1½" x 40" and one strip each 1" x 40".

**Black:** Cut one strip 9" x 40". Cut a 9" square from this strip, and cut the remainder into 1½" and 2" strips.
(You may need additional strips, depending upon the width of the fabric and patchwork.)

**Lining fabric:** ⅝ yard of silk brocade.

**Bias binding for edging:** Cut bias strips from purple silk. Bias can be cut 1½" wide; you will need about 90" of purple, in addition to the plaid bias already cut. (I cut bias from the fabric and sew enough strips together to make up the needed length.)

**Foundation fabric:** ⅝ yard. Use prewashed white cotton flannel or natural-colored muslin; the patchwork will be sewn to this foundation.

**Narrow ribbon in jewel tones:** approximately 3" each of about five colors.

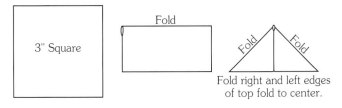

1" folded to ½"

## Folded Fabric Overlay

When you want to piece a narrow bar of color in the patchwork, you will find it easier to use a folded fabric overlay than to piece the silk. With a hot iron, fold the ruby red and the orange 1" strips in half lengthwise to make ½" strips. Fold one 1½" purple strip lengthwise to make a ¾" strip.

## Folded Triangle

Cut two squares from the 3" purple strip. Press the squares in half and fold down the right and left edges of the fold to meet in the middle, creating a folded triangle.

| 3" Square | Fold | |
| --- | --- | --- |

Fold right and left edges of top fold to center.

## Making the Sections

Following is a variation of the basic vest in *Pieced Clothing* VARIATIONS (pages 6 and 24); the dipping front curved edge is added by extending the pattern piece 1½" at the center front. Draw a gentle curve from the bottom of the front lower edge to the edge of the side seam.

[If you need a smaller or larger size, add at least 2" to your bust measurement. Look in a mirror to determine the width of your center panel with a tape measure (inside armhole to inside armhole). Since the front and back panels are the same width, subtract their combined measurement from your adjusted bust measurement. Divide the remaining amount in half to determine the width of each side panel. For waist length, measure from shoulder to waist for the length of the center panels. Depth of the armhole is from shoulder to underarm, plus an extra inch or two for ease. Subtract the armhole depth from the length of the center panel to determine the length of the side panels, and add seam allowance to all pieces before cutting.]

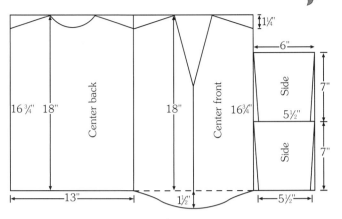

Dimensions of pattern pieces

Cut the vest pattern pieces from the flannel or muslin foundation fabric. **Add seam allowance** to the pieces, and a little extra if you are afraid of distorting the pattern with your machine piecing. You can trim the pattern pieces to size after piecing.

All silk strips will be sewn to the foundation. Begin piecing on the center back. Position your black triangle (#1) on the foundation. Pin the first strip (#2) on one edge of the triangle, right sides together, matching the point of the triangle with the edge of the strip. Sew the seam and press out the strip, then trim the long end of the strip. Because you are working on the diagonal, **do not cut the strip while it is wrong side over the triangle**. Continue adding strips to both sides of the triangle until the whole pattern piece is covered with strips. Make tiny bows from narrow ribbon; sew them to the black triangle and to the points of the folded triangles.

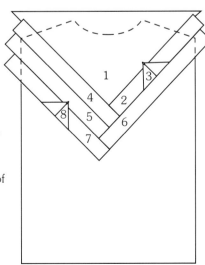

Begin with a 9" square that has been cut into triangles.

Add folded triangle as overlay on raw edge of #2: strip #6 secures the triangle in seam.

After piecing: Sew ribbon bows on points of triangle to secure. Sew bows to black triangle.

Now proceed to sew the patchwork strips to the center fronts and the two side panels, in the same manner as described above, and using the drawings as guides.

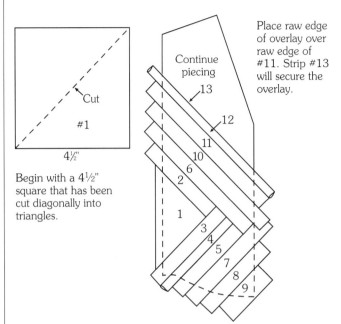

Begin with a 4½" square that has been cut diagonally into triangles.

Place raw edge of overlay over raw edge of #11. Strip #13 will secure the overlay.

## Assembling the Vest

Place the patchwork pieces, wrong sides together, over the lining fabric. Place the vest pattern over the patchwork pieces and trim them to the correct size. Cut the lining at the same time, so it will be the same size as the patchwork. Since silk ravels, this approach eliminates trying to match up the raw edges of the lining with the patchwork. Nevertheless, handle the silk as little as possible.

You will cover all the raw edges with bias binding *except* the inside lining shoulder seams. You can piece the bias binding using both the purple and plaid bias strips.

For the front tie, fold a strip of fabric in half lengthwise, wrong sides together, and sew into a tube. Turn it right side out and hand hem one end. The ties are 7" long and the raw end is sewn onto the front binding.

To finish the shoulder seams, sew both layers of the center back, including the lining, to the center front layers. Exclude the lining, then hand sew the front panel lining over the shoulder seam. Bind the center front and around the neck opening with bias binding. Pin binding to the vest seam, matching the raw edges, and sew the binding and vest seams together. Press the binding over the seam and fold in the raw edge of the binding to meet the raw edge of the seam. Fold the binding again and pin it over the seam line. Slip stitch the folded edge of the binding over the seam line.

Sew the side panels to the center panel with bias binding over the seam. Pin the side panels to the center panel, starting at the waist edge, with lining sides together. This binding also finishes the armhole. Finish the lower edge of the vest with bias grain binding.

♥ With four adult children and eight grandchildren, at Christmas time we have a steady stream of visitors. They come and go depending upon their schedules for extended families. We have settled into a program of having the whole family for Christmas dinner in odd-numbered years, so they can dine with their other parents in the even-numbered ones. We do have a traditional dinner, but I also like to have several types of nut breads on hand for morning snacks or surprise drop-ins. This bread was a favorite of my mother, Mary Bechis; here is her original recipe.

# Raw Apple, Date, and Walnut Cake

Chop 1 cup of apples and 1 cup of dates. Place them in a bowl with 1 teaspoon of baking soda and 1 cup of boiling water. Set this aside to cool.

Cream together 1 cup of white sugar, a quarter-pound of butter or shortening, 1 egg, and 1 teaspoon of vanilla.

Add to the creamed mixture 1½ cups of flour, 1 teaspoon of salt, and 1 cup of chopped walnuts. Now add the apple-date mixture. Blend together and place in a greased and floured 1½ quart (4" x 8" x 3") loaf pan. Bake at 350° for 50-60 minutes, until it tests done. Cool the loaf in the pan before turning it out.

# MOLLY MILLIGAN-COKELEY

## Father Christmas

Molly Cokeley's doll-making classes at The Cotton Patch in Lafayette, California, fill before the ink is dry on the brochures! Her dolls have her own fun-filled, enthusiastic, optimistic personality. She also owns a pattern company with the appropriate name Professor Silver Threads. My grandchildren believe that my dolls come to life at night, and they can be sure that Molly's Santa knows whether they've been good or bad. Molly is also currently organizing a series of seminars, with top dollmaking teachers, to take place several times a year in the Santa Cruz Mountains. You can be sure I will be there to learn and laugh, and I expect to see you there, too.

### Materials Needed

- Face—scrap of cotton Lycra™ (⅛ yard)
- Needle—a 4" needle for assistance in sculpting the face
- Pigma Micron™ colored pens—for the eyes
- Berol Prismacolor® pencils—for face color and shadows
- Matte medium—to seal the face color
- Raw wool, roving, etc. for the beard
- Body—½ yard of muslin
- Stuffing—16 oz. bag: I prefer to use a slippery stuffing like Soft Touch®
- Quilting thread—to sew the body parts to the torso
- Pants—½ yard of lightweight wool (A pair of old wool slacks work wonders.)
- Patches on pants—two scraps of fabric, of a color that is of the same value as the pants
- Vest—½ yard of lightweight wool (Again, a pair of old slacks is great.) This is not lined, so make sure that the weave is tight, or use your embroidery to keep it from unraveling.
- Embroidery floss—for the vest (Feel free to use as many colors as you like. I suggest keeping them earthy.)
- Buttons for the vest—I used 2 old brass buttons, ⅜" diameter.
- Sleeves and vest insert on chest—Use an old sweater turned inside out, or ⅛ yard of wool knit.
- Mittens—ribbing of old sweater or socks (or ⅛ yard of light wool knit)
- Metallic thread—to sew bells to wrist
- Six tiny bells—dangling at the wrist
- Boots—15" x 15" piece of soft leather
- Waxed linen thread—to sew the boots
- Dark shoe polish—to make the boots look scuffed and worn
- Old toothbrush—to apply shoe polish to boots

MERRY CHRISTMAS

- Cape—¾ yard of heavy wool (an old coat) or upholstery fabric
- Cape lining—¾ yard of satin-like coat lining
- Velvet ribbon—39" for bottom of cape
- Cording—⅓ yard of cording to tie the cape on
- Fur—a piece ½" x 39", may be pieced (I found an old piece of ermine that worked well for the bottom of the cape.)
- Berries—I used nine clumps of ½"-diameter berries around the bottom of the cape.
- Wood dowel—$\frac{7}{16}$" diameter, 19" long (to be trimmed later)
- Block of wood, tree stump, anything a drill can go through, for the stand

## EMBELLISHMENTS

- 4 birds—one for tip of hood, one on the hand, two in the nest
- 1 bird's nest—may be purchased, or made of found and dried grasses and weeds with small blossoms. Work materials while still green.
- 1 twig nest carrier—purchased at a dried-flower shop. A small basket will work.

## Pattern Directions

The pattern line is your stitch line. Unless otherwise noted, trace all pattern pieces before cutting. It is best to use template plastic. Trace the patterns onto the plastic using a fine-point permanent marker: others smear. Cut the templates at the traced line. Using the templates, trace the pattern shapes directly onto the wrong side of the fabric. Add the seam allowance beyond the traced line, and cut at the seam allowance line. Stitch your pieces together, right sides together, and clip curves where necessary. Turn right side out.

## STUFFING HINTS

Don't jam the stuffing; tamp it, as you would in setting a plant in soil. Always stuff down the center of the cavity. Rather than using little bits, I tend to stuff with large pieces and continually feed it into the cavity. This helps to keep a smooth finish.

## BODY

When constructing the body, think of the body position: express the action of the figure by the positioning of the arms, legs, and head in relation to the torso.

1. Stuff the torso, arms, and one leg firmly, but not rock-hard.
2. On the other leg, open the seam at the heel to insert the dowel. Push the dowel through this opening, to the full length of the leg.
3. Stuff the heel first. Then stuff the foot. Pin the opening of the toe closed. Stuff the doweled leg, lightly circling the dowel with stuffing and then tamping the stuffing evenly around the dowel until it is firm. Be careful of air pockets. Leave the top open.
4. Bring the doweled leg up to the torso, so the leg is pressed against the body, not sticking straight out. Note the side of the hip protrusion. The outside of the thigh should meet at the protrusion of the hip. Make a mark where the dowel meets the torso. Move from that mark slightly in front of the seam, and cut an X in the torso. Be sure not to cut the seam threads.
5. Insert the dowel up into the stuffed torso. You may have to twist the dowel or re-stuff around it so that the torso stands straight on the leg. Think of your own body and how your leg looks at your hip joint.
6. Turn the fabric under and pin the top of the thigh to the protrusion of the hip. Turn the raw edge under and pin, making a smooth arc. Continue to press the leg to the body so that you start to form the beginning of the crotch. You'll find that, in this area, the raw edges naturally get buried because of the pressing of the leg to the body. Check to make sure that the leg looks normal in this position.
7. Repeat the positioning process for the other leg. At this time decide what motion you want this leg to maintain. If you want him to be taking a step, rotate the leg (as if at the hip joint) so that it moves back. Pin it in place. Pin at the top of the thigh first, then the back of the leg to hold its position, then in the crotch, to bring the leg in towards the body.
8. Check for the following:
   a. The legs should be the same length.

b. They should look natural, coming off the body at the hip joint.

c. If you turn the body upside down, the joinery at the hips should line up evenly. Make sure one isn't ahead of the other, or higher than the other.
You may have to do some re-pinning.

9. On the leg that is moving back, bend behind the knee and pin. Take a tuck at the back of the knee to take the stiffness out of the leg.

10. Once you are satisfied with the positioning of the legs, sew the legs to the torso, using quilting thread for strength.

11. Sew the torso closed at the neck.

12. Take a dart in the small of the back to give some curvature to the torso.

13. Set the arms aside.

When making this doll, you are creating an illusion. Some of the clothes are sewn onto the body of the doll.

## PANTS

1. Sew up the inseam on both legs. Turn one leg right side out and place it inside the other leg. Now you have two right sides together. Match the inseam, pin up the front and back seams, and sew them.

2. Turn the pants so that both legs are right side out. If you prefer, cut patches for the pants from the scrap fabric and add to the pants. Slip the pants on to the body of the doll.

3. Pin the front seam of the pants to the center of the torso. Do the same for the back. On one side of the body, pull the fabric out to find the middle of the remaining fabric, and pin that to the side seam of the torso. Do the same on the other side of the body.

4. Make a box pleat in the front and back with the excess fabric. Pin to the body.

5. Whip stitch pants into place, using double thread. (The raw edge of the top of the pants will be hidden by the vest.)

6. Using a running stitch, gather the bottom of each pant leg and tie off. Do not attach to the leg. (The raw edge of this leg will be tucked into the top of the boot.)

## VEST

1. Embroider your design onto the vest fabric.

2. Wrap the vest fabric around to the front of the torso. Smooth in the back and pin at the back of the shoulders. Continue to manipulate the fabric to the front of the chest. Fold under the raw edges in the front and pin closed at the waist. (This hides the raw edges of the pants.) At this point, shorten or lengthen the vest. Angle the front of the vest into a V on the chest. From your sweater fabric, cut a piece that is big enough to be inserted in the V spot under the vest (about 3" x 3½"). Whip stitch it into place, then pin down the vest in front. Trim the excess fabric at the top of the vest and at the shoulder area. Turn the raw edges under and stitch them down across the shoulders. Tack the buttons to the center front of the vest.

## ARMS

1. Place the top of one stuffed arm on the shoulder (the same side of the body as the dowel leg). Turn under the raw edges of the arm. Rotate the arm to a forward position. The thumb should be on the upper side. Push the arm close to the body. Here you will notice that the under-arm fabric will naturally be pressed between the arm and the torso. Be sure that the rest of the muslin edges have been turned under, forming a smooth arc as you pin.

2. On the inside of the elbow, bend the arm and take a tuck to remove the stiffness from the arm.

3. The other arm is going to hold the bird. Again place the arm, with the raw edges turned under, at the shoulder point. Rotate the arm so that the hand is held high. Follow the same instructions as for the first arm. Make a bend and tuck at the elbow, and again at the wrist.

## SLEEVE

Zigzag stitch the edges of the two sleeves to keep them from unraveling. Then sew the seams and turn. Place the seams under the arm as you slip the sleeves onto the arm. Cover the muslin joinery

at the shoulder as you pin in place. Whip stitch onto the body.

## SLEEVE CAP

Here you use two pieces 8½" x 3¾", one for each arm. For each, sew the two short sides together to form a loop. Turn it right side out. Fold in half, bringing the raw edges together. Turn so the raw edges are on the inside of the tube, then pin. Whip stitch the edges together with tiny stitches, and close. Remove the pins. Slide the piece up the arm so that the sleeve cap will cover the sweater joinery. Ladder stitch this into place. Repeat for the other arm.

## MITTENS

Using the hand template again, trace it onto the wrong side of the material and sew the mitten seams. Then cut it out, leaving the wrist areas open. Work them onto the hands. Using the metallic thread, attach the bells to the wrists, just below the mitten edges.

## BOOTS

1. Sew the back seam of the boot sleeve, right sides together, and turn. Slip it onto the leg, with the cap facing the toe and the seam at the heel.
2. Tuck the pants inside.
3. Sew the back seam of the boot top, right sides together, and turn. Slip it onto the foot so that the cap of the boot sleeve is on the top side. (No need to sew these two pieces together.) Push the boot sleeve down so it looks like it's sagging onto the boot top, keeping the pants tucked in.
4. Whip stitch the sole of the boot to the top of the boot, using small, even stitches. I used waxed linen thread and then applied acrylic paint to hide it. Lightly brush dark shoe polish around the boot top, and a little up onto the boot sleeve: this gives the effect of old, worn boots. Rub the polish in to take away sharp edges. Apply lightly: you can always add more.

## Sculpting the Face

### HINTS

Use pins to mark the face. Halfway between the forehead and the chin is where you place the eyes. The tip of the nose is halfway between the eyes and the chin. Halfway between the nose and the chin is the opening of the mouth.

Start each feature by tying a knot in the end of the thread. A few overlapping stitches in the back of the head secure the knot so that it won't pull through the fabric. Since you are working with fabric, the stuffing and the thread create a three-dimensional face. Because there will be tension on your thread, I recommend that you pinch the fabric gently into position, then pull the thread to retain that tension. Do one feature at a time and tie off the thread by using a sequence of overlapping stitches; then tie a knot.

Make sure you have a very long thread. I use a single strand, but you may want to start with a double one until you get the feel.

Use a couch stitch to stabilize the thread for the flare and bridge of the nose.

For sculpting the face, I basically use a standard needle. However, I do switch to a 4" needle when necessary to pass completely through the head.

### NOSE

1. Start with the flare of the nostrils. Make sure you have plenty of stuffing in the nose. You can adjust the stuffing with your needle. With the long needle, enter the back of the head just below where a hat would sit on your head. Go through the head and come out at point 1. Insert the needle at point 2, exit at point 3, enter at point 4, exit at point 1. Leaving the threads loose, mark the flare of the nostril with pins.

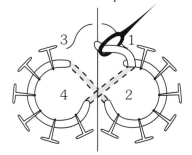

Mark flair of nose with pins

2. Gently, with the thread on the outside of the pins, tighten the threads so that they begin to form the flare. Go through the nose with your needle from point 1 back to point 3. Do this three times. This secures the tension. You should be back at point 1. Re-enter at point 1 and couch stitch the flare thread on the opposite side (point 3) of the nose, with the needle exiting on the opposite side (point 1) of the nose ready to take the next couch stitch. Repeat this process until you get to the nostrils, about three times on each side of the flare.

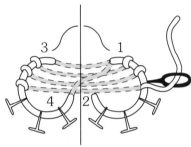

3. Take the needle through one nostril (on the side you have ended on) and exit through the back of the head. You have now made a stitch creating the nostril. Pull slightly. Enter the head again, exiting the other nostril; take a stitch and exit the back of the head, pulling the thread to create the other nostril. When you are satisfied, take a couple of locking stitches and tie off.

## Bridge of Nose

1. Insert the needle from the back of the head and exit at point 5, enter at point 1, exit at point 3, enter at point 6, and exit the back of the head. Gently pinch the bridge of the nose, then pull the thread to create the bridge. When you are satisfied with the bridge, making sure that it looks smooth, take a couple of stitches in the back of the head to secure the tension. Then enter the back of the head, exit at point 1, and re-enter at the same point.

2. Begin your couching on the opposite side of the nose, as you did with the flare of the nostril. Continue to the end of the bridge, exit

at the back of the head, and secure with a knot.

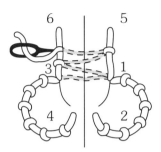

## EYES

The space between the eyes is the same size as the eye.

1. Mark with pins the tear duct, then the corner of the eye, then the pupil. With a brown pen, mark the pupil and remove the pin.

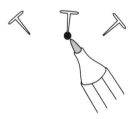

2. With a brown pen, make a dotted circle evenly around the pupil. This is the iris.

3. Make a dotted line from the tear duct to the top of the iris, then one from the top of the iris to the corner of the eye. Do the same for the bottom lid. Repeat the steps for the other eye.

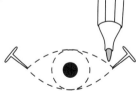

## Coloring the Face

Use the colored pencils, which are soft and blend easily. Always use the side of your pencil to avoid sharp lines. Color his whole face except the eyes. Add shadows, and blush his nose and cheeks. I find that using earth tones for this character works well. Do not be afraid to use plum colors, blues, etc.

Remember, start out lightly. You can always add more color later. When you have gotten the flesh tones and eye shadows to your satisfaction, seal his face with a matte finish. Do not seal the eyeball area yet. If you want to add more color, you can do it over the matte finish. Dry it with a hair dryer for fast results. After it is completely dry, seal the eyeball area.

## EYES AGAIN

When you start coloring the eyes, use as many colors as you want and lightly draw from the circumference of the iris to the center of the pupil. Leave one tiny spot without color, to create a highlight.

highlight

The top of the iris should be darker, to suggest the shadow of the lid. Frame the iris with a band of color and re-draw the pupils with black. Draw lashes with the Pigma pens.

## Attaching the Head

Tuck the neck edges under to the length of neck desired, and press it to the body on the shoulder line. Tilt the head from side to side and back and forth to determine the angle at which you prefer his head. Think about what the position says: a head tilted at an angle suggests curiosity. When you have decided the posturing of the head, pin it into place and sew, using the quilting thread for strength. Don't let the head wobble: it may need more stuffing or a shorter neck.

Divide the roving into sections for the hair, mustache, beard, and eyebrows, using whatever lengths you prefer. Glue the roving sections to the head.

## Additional Clothing

### CAPE

This is the only piece of clothing that is made to come off your Santa. Thus, you can make different capes for different seasons.

1. Cut one cape piece 36" x 20" and one lining piece 36" x 19". The lining is smaller to force the sides of the cape to turn under ½" (to look like a facing).
2. Sew the shorter sides of the lining and cape together and one long edge, right sides together. Turn right side out.
3. Fold the side edges so the seam is ½" from the edge, creating a mock facing. Take small tack stitches on both sides, along the seam, to hold the facing in place.
4. Using a running stitch, gather the top of the cape to approximately 4". Set aside; do not tie it off.
5. Add the fur trim, velvet ribbon, and berries to the bottom edge of cape.

### HOOD

1. With right sides facing, sew the top seams of the hood together. Repeat for the lining pieces.
2. Turn the hood right side out and place the lining outside the hood, right sides together.
3. Sew the front sides together. Then turn the lining inside the hood.
4. Match the length of the gathered cape edge to the neck of the hood. Tie it off.
5. Place the outside of the hood against the outside of the cape. Sew only the outer cape fabrics together.
6. Turn under the lining and sew the lining of the hood down to the lining of the cape.
7. Center and whip stitch the cord to the outside of the cape, on the seam where the hood meets the cape. Trim the tails to the desired length.

## Base

Center Father Christmas atop the base, marking the position of the dowel. Trim the dowel to 1" below the boot. Drill a 1" hole into the base.

## Embellishing

Construct the bird's nest, and tack on the birds as shown in the photo. I only glue whatever can't be sewn on. Have fun, be creative, be you.

❤ Every Christmas since I was a little girl, there was a very small Christmas tree at both my grand-mothers' homes. They decorated them with bits of jewelry for the sparkle, miniature dolls, German ornaments, etc. I have combined these two trees and added my own small things. There is now an old electric toy train, and a toyland that has been created from small toys from my childhood and the childhoods of my husband, Craig, and my children Tyler and Kirsten. Every year I look forward to this timeless treasure. It's like seeing old friends, who are really all the memories this tree stirs up.

# Dressed-up Unloved Sweet Potatoes
### Serves 8

2 cups of cooked, mashed sweet potatoes
½ tsp. butter
½ tsp. salt
Add a little warm cream and mix these ingredients together.

8 large cooking apples (pippin apples are wonderful)
Cut in half between the stem and the bottom of the apple.
Remove the seeds.
Remove the pulp, leaving a ½" wall of apple.
Chop the pulp and add to the potatoes.

Roll the apple shells in butter, then in brown sugar.
Fill the apples with the potato mixture.
Roll again in butter, then brown sugar.
Bake in a greased baking dish at 300° for at least 1½ hours,
    basting with apple juice.

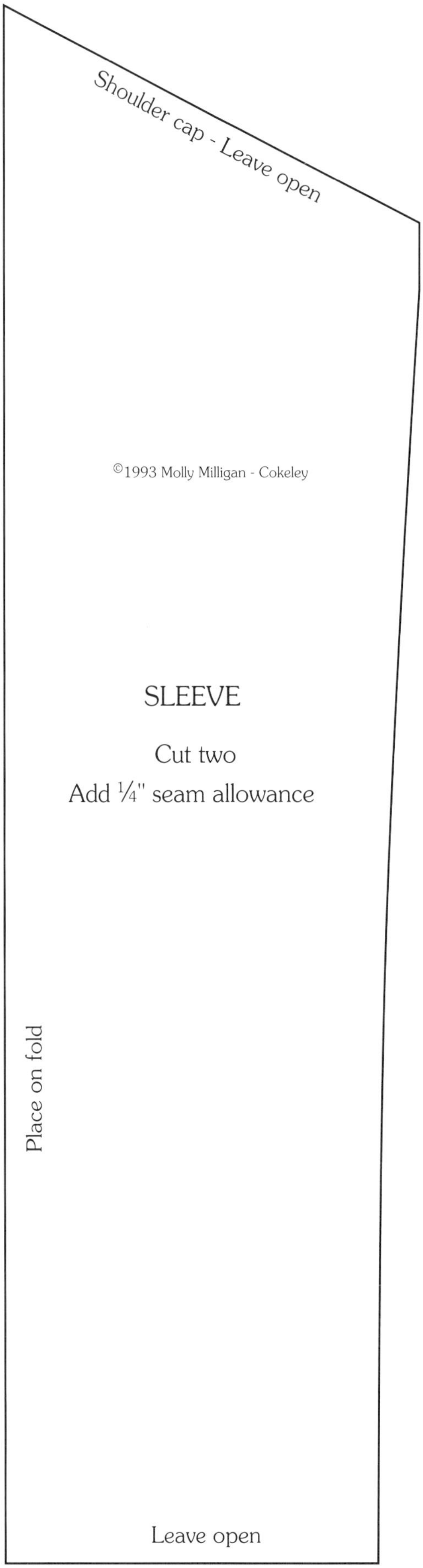

Shoulder cap - Leave open

©1993 Molly Milligan - Cokeley

SLEEVE

Cut two

Add ¼" seam allowance

Place on fold

Leave open

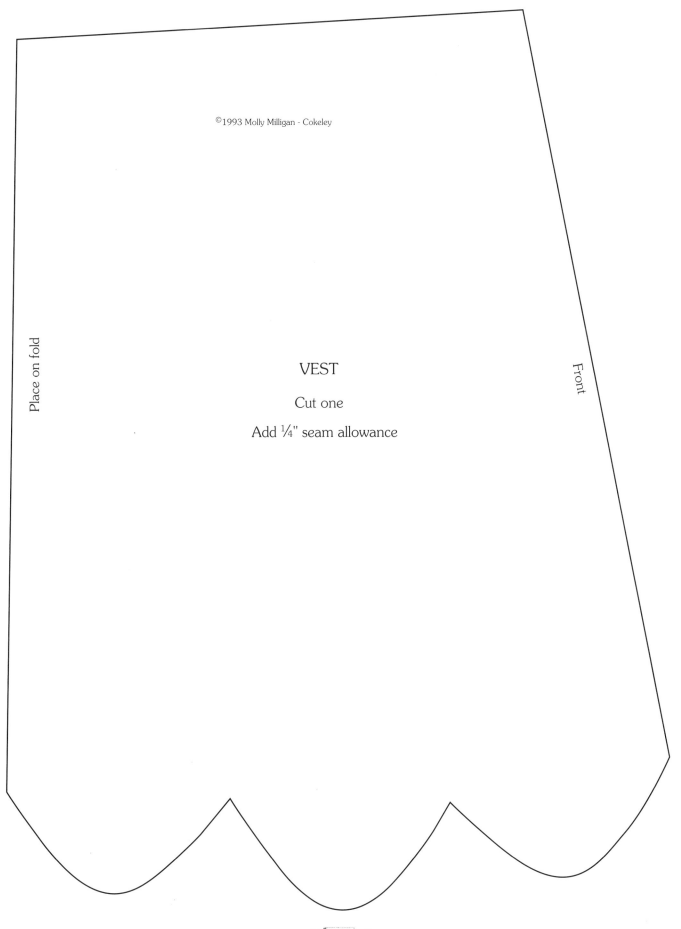

Place on fold

VEST

Cut one

Add ¼" seam allowance

Front

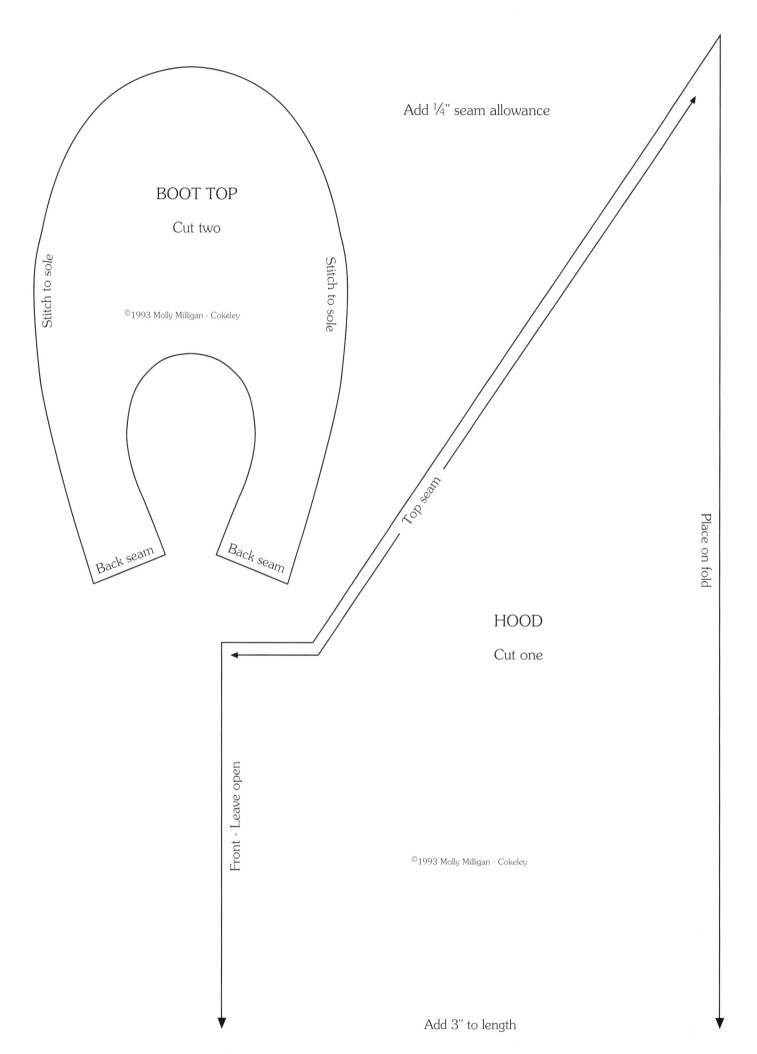

BOOT TOP

Cut two

Stitch to sole

Stitch to sole

©1993 Molly Milligan - Cokeley

Back seam

Back seam

Add ¼" seam allowance

Top seam

Place on fold

HOOD

Cut one

Front - Leave open

©1993 Molly Milligan - Cokeley

Add 3" to length

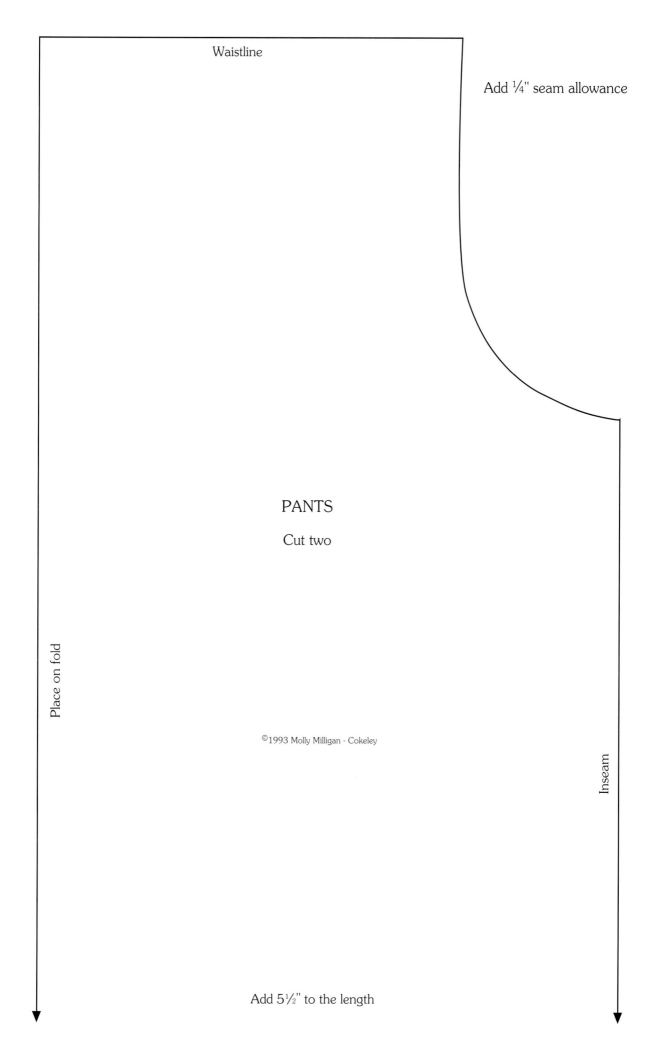

Waistline

Add ¼" seam allowance

PANTS

Cut two

Place on fold

Inseam

©1993 Molly Milligan - Cokeley

Add 5½" to the length

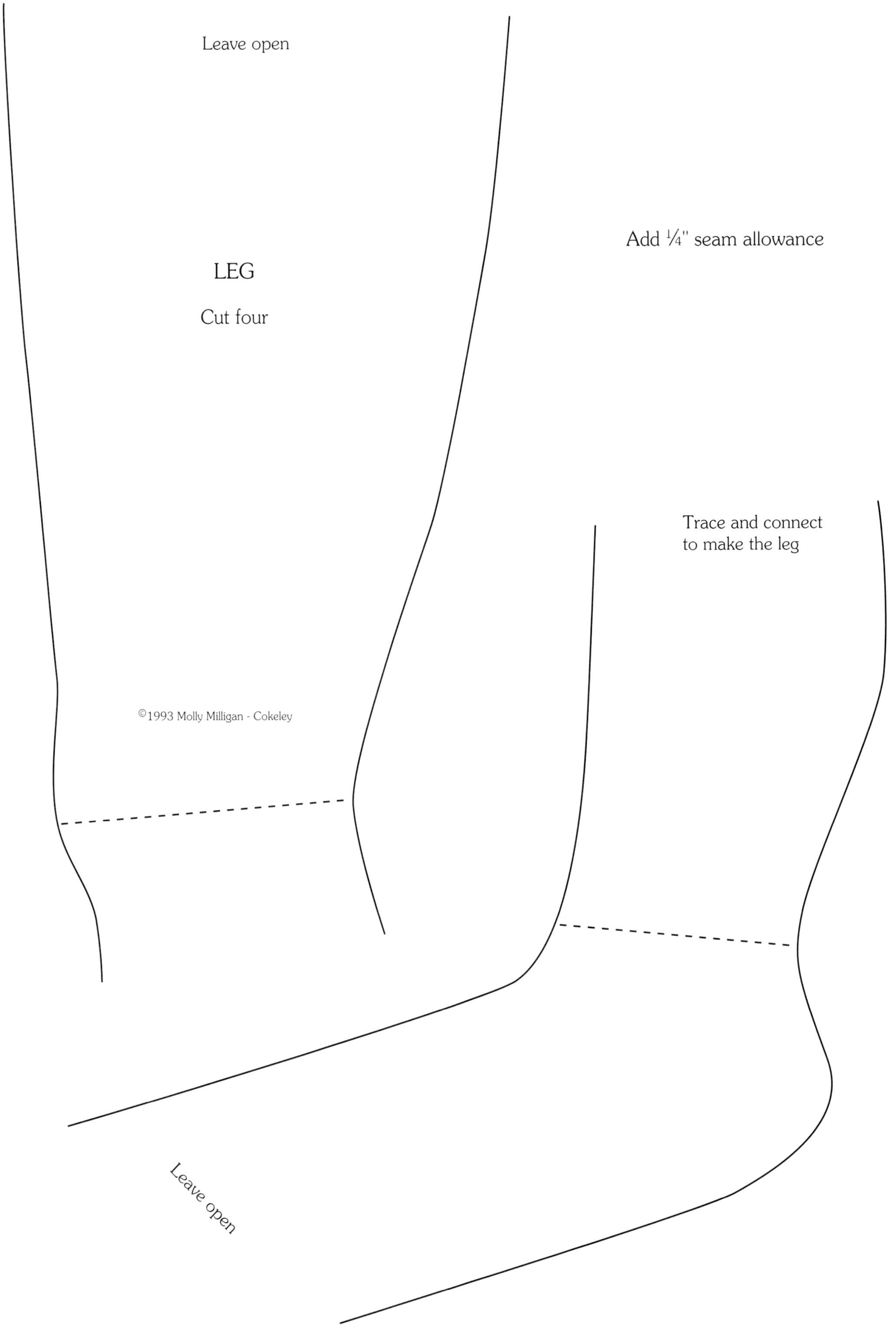

Leave open
Add ¼" seam allowance
LEG
Cut four
Trace and connect
to make the leg
©1993 Molly Milligan - Cokeley
Leave open

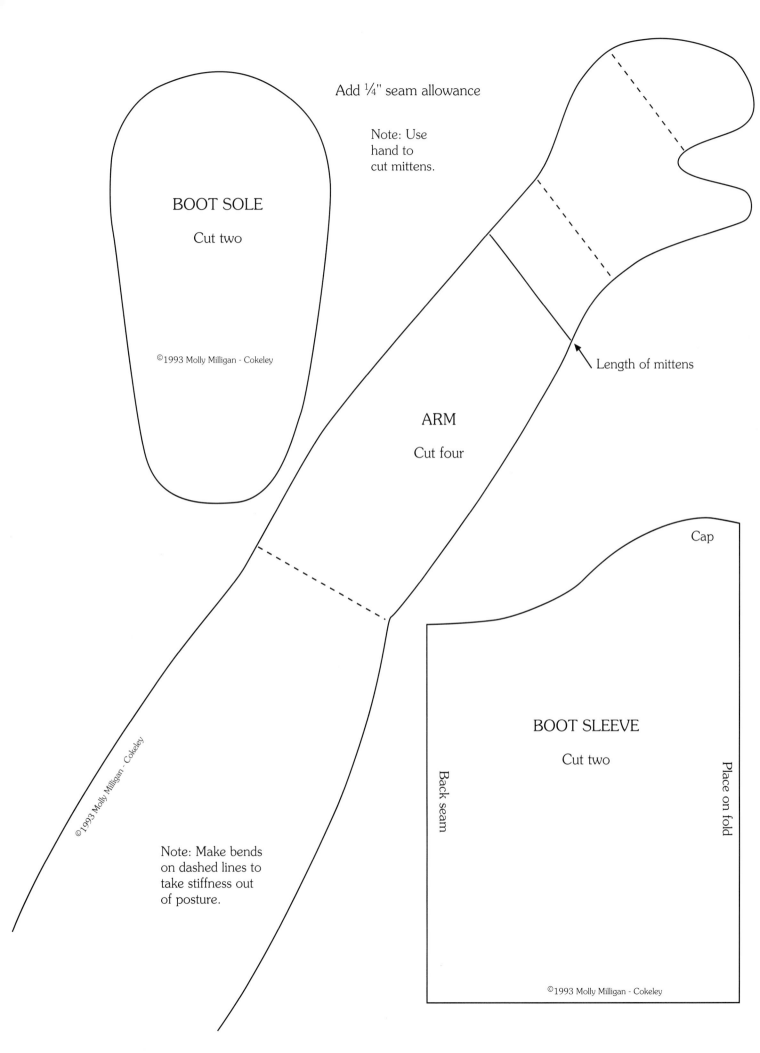

BOOT SOLE

Cut two

©1993 Molly Milligan - Cokeley

Add ¼" seam allowance

Note: Use
hand to
cut mittens.

Length of mittens

ARM

Cut four

©1993 Molly Milligan - Cokeley

Note: Make bends
on dashed lines to
take stiffness out
of posture.

Cap

BOOT SLEEVE

Cut two

Back seam

Place on fold

©1993 Molly Milligan - Cokeley

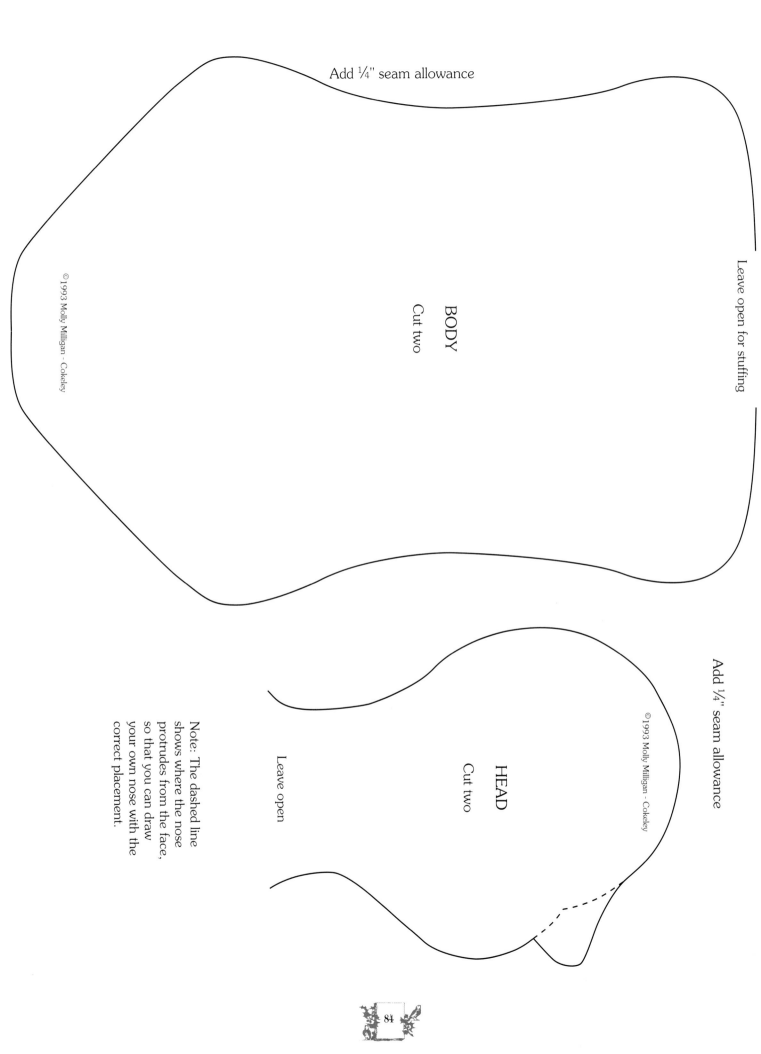

Add ¼" seam allowance

Leave open for stuffing

BODY
Cut two

© 1993 Molly Milligan - Cokeley

Add ¼" seam allowance

© 1993 Molly Milligan - Cokeley

HEAD
Cut two

Leave open

Note: The dashed line
shows where the nose
protrudes from the face,
so that you can draw
your own nose with the
correct placement.

# NICKI BECKER

*I have known Nicki Becker since the early days of Quilt Market, because she taught classes at Karey Bresenhan's Houston shop Great Expectations. I still look for her as soon as I arrive at Market each fall. Nicki has the rare talent of making "cute" work. Her creations have a simplicity that makes them ideal projects to do with your children and grandchildren. This wonderful Christmas stocking gives you a taste of her love for fabric, paint, and needle crafting.*

## Folk Art Santa Stocking

### Materials Needed

- ½ yard of osnaburg or muslin
- ½ yard of printed fabric for backing and lining
- 5 Stencil-ease® stencil brushes
- Stencil-ease Fab-Tex® paints: golden honey, dark green, cranberry, white, and black
- Pigma Micron™ 01 or Pilot® ultra-fine permanent pens: black and red
- Freezer paper or waxed stencil paper or Mylar®
- Sharp scissors or X-Acto® knife
- Paper towels
- Masking tape
- Cutting mat

### Assembly

You need to make five separate stencils for the Santa, two for the checkerboard cuff, and two for the toe. For a one-time project, freezer paper makes the easiest and most economical stencils; the other suggested materials are better if you expect to make many stockings. (If you use either of the others, you will tape the stencil to the fabric, rather than ironing.)

Trace each pattern onto the unwaxed side of the freezer paper, leaving about 2" around each pattern. Working on a piece of glass or a rotary-cutter mat, cut the color area from each pattern. Try to make one continuous cut, turning the paper rather than lifting the knife; each time you start and stop, you might create a jagged edge. You can correct mistakes with cellophane tape.

If you have never stenciled before, practice first by cutting a simple shape, such as a heart or circle, from the freezer paper. Iron the pattern, waxed side down, to a scrap of the fabric you will be using. Lay several sheets of newspaper under the fabric to absorb excess paint. Since stenciling requires a dry brush, you will need a separate one for each color. Dip the brush into the paint and dab it onto a paper towel to work the paint up into the fibers, and to

remove excess paint. When the brush is almost dry, start at the outer edge of the pattern and work toward the center, applying the paint with a circular motion: the edges will be darker than the center. As you need more paint, repeat the towel procedure. To make a darker color, stencil again: do not overload your brush. (A kneaded eraser is sometimes successful in removing a light drip quickly.) Remember that much of the charm of stenciling is the folk-art irregular shading. The paint is absorbed into the fibers quickly, so you can move to the next stencil almost immediately.

When you feel confident about your stenciling, start the stocking. Trace the stocking shape onto a 12" x 16" piece of muslin, but do not cut it out yet. Make a stencil for the #1 cuff color, following the stocking pattern and leaving ¼" around the edges for the seam allowance. Iron the stencil to the fabric. Stencil all the squares, then peel the paper off and carefully align and repeat the sequence for the #2 cuff color. Stencil and remove, then do the toe checkerboard. Make stencils for each of the remaining colors and shapes. Place the Santa as shown on the pattern layout, iron, and stencil. Repeat with the other stencils, aligning them carefully, as shown on the pattern layout.

Allow all stenciling to dry for a few hours, then set with a hot, dry iron. It is now safe for gentle washing. With a marking pen, outline the design: small dashed lines create a nice finishing touch. With the black pen draw the mustache, bottom of the beard, and eye lines; draw the mouth in red.

If you wish to outline quilt the stocking, do so before assembly. Then cut the stocking out and, using it as a pattern, cut one backing piece and two lining pieces. Sew the front lining to the stocking front across the top only, right sides together. Repeat for the back piece. Press seams flat. Lay the two pieces right sides together and stitch, leaving a 4" opening in the lining. Turn, then stitch the opening closed and push the lining down into the stocking. Sew a ribbon loop to the top left corner for hanging.

❤ One of our family Christmas traditions is to attend church on Christmas Eve, then return home to snacks and our gift exchange. This is one of our favorite snacks.

# Frosty Yule Log

- 8 oz. of cream cheese
- Milk
- 1 packet of your favorite dry dip mix (French onion, onion and bacon, or garlic and olive work well)
- Two 4½ oz. cans of deviled ham
- 1 cup of chopped walnuts or pecans
- Pimento strip
- 1 bag of king-sized corn chips

1. Soften the cream cheese with a little milk. Divide the mixture in half. Spread one half into a 3" x 6" strip on a serving tray.
2. Combine the dry dip mix with the two cans of deviled ham. Form this into a 6" roll and place it atop the cream cheese strip.
3. Using the remaining cream cheese, frost the top of the roll. Cover with chopped nuts. Form pimento strip into a bow and garnish log.
   Serve with corn chips.

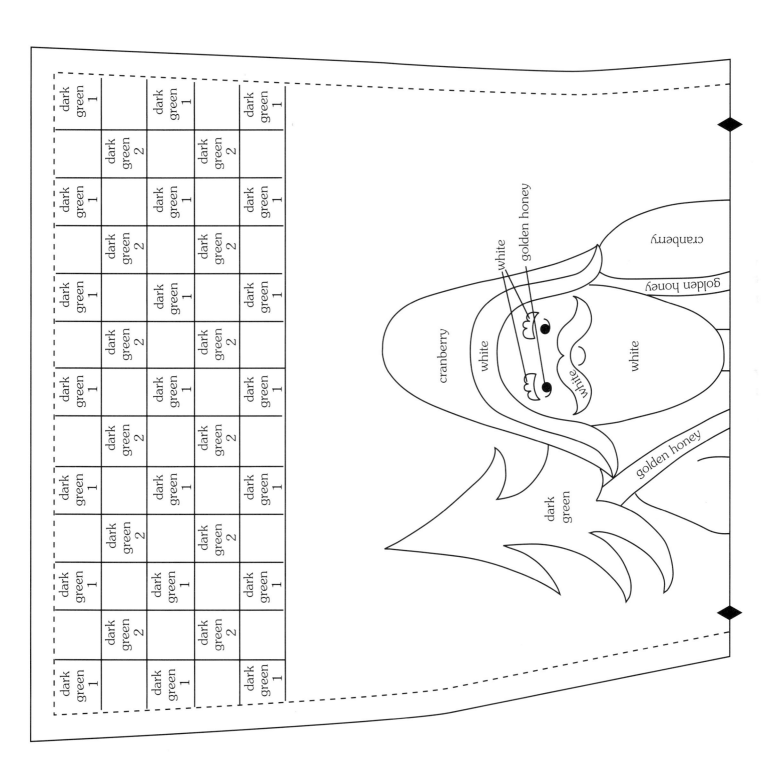

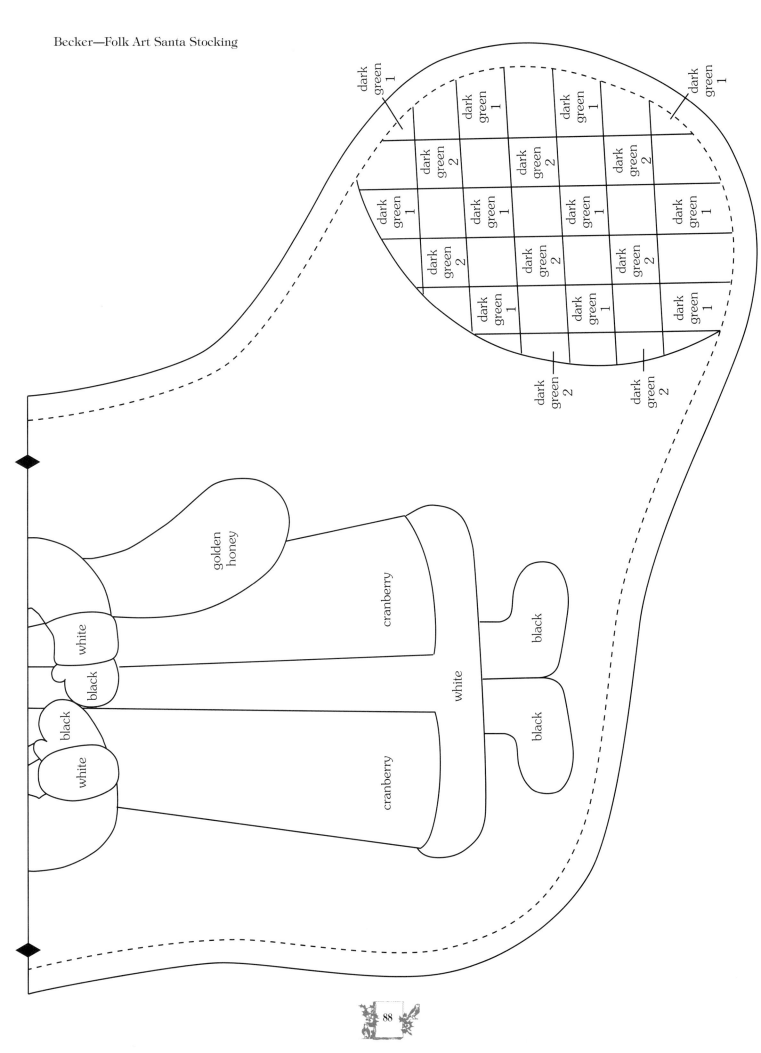

# CATHIE I. HOOVER

*Cathie Hoover lives officially in Modesto, California, but she is known as the Cow Lady of Moo-desto! She has her own wearable art company, and I proudly own two of her garments — but I have learned not to wear them to the grocery, since the ice cream melts while you answer all the questions from other shoppers about where and how. Cathie lectures, teaches, and organizes a jacket contest each year for the Empty Spools Seminar. Her humor pervades everything she does. In her "spare" time, besides doing incredibly detailed cross stitching and making quilts to decorate her husband's large dental office, Cathie also lovingly tends over one hundred rose bushes.*

## Whimsical Cow Christmas Tree Skirt

*Finished size is 81" diameter.*

### Materials Needed

- 4½ yards of 54"-width pink plaid for the tree skirt
- 1 yard of black-and-white spotted fabric for the cows
- ⅛ yard of pink fabric for the cows' udders
- ⅝ yard of green moiré fabric for the trees
- 1½ yards of burgundy moiré for the binding and ties
- ¼ yard of gold tricot lamé for the stars
- ⅛ yard of silver tricot lamé for the moon
- ⅛ yard total of red and pink tricot lamé for the tree stars
- 4 yards of ⅜"-wide red and green striped ribbon for the bows
- Twelve 18 mm gold cow bells
- 12 small brass round-headed studs for cows' eyes
- 1½ yards of Wonder Under™
- 2 packages (or equivalent yardage) of Totally Stable® (an iron-on stabilizer for appliqué work)
- Fray Check™
- 1½ yards of 36"-wide freezer paper (for tracing)
- Yardstick

Thread to match or contrast, as you prefer. I used 100% cotton quilting thread for the blanket stitch on the cows and Sulky® size 40 rayon metallic thread for all lamé appliqué.

Selvage

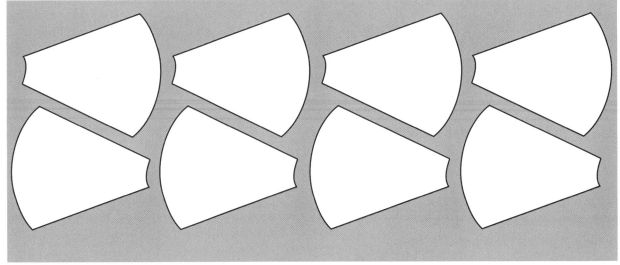

Selvage

## Assembly

1. Trace the skirt pattern onto one end of the freezer paper, extending the left and right sides as indicated. Measure 31" from the arrow tip of the pattern top to get the point of the bottom curve. At this point, fold the pattern in half lengthwise and draw the bottom curve. *Option:* If you wish to make a skirt of only 59" diameter, repeat the procedure but measure 20" from the center arrow tip and 15" from the side arrow tips. Use ½" seam allowance when sewing the fabric: the seam allowance is included in the pattern.

2. If you are using a plaid fabric, arrange the patterns so that you will be able to match the bias edge with any pattern on the fabric. Cut out eight wedges from skirt fabric. Cut 5"-wide bias strips from the binding fabric. Fold strips in half lengthwise, wrong sides facing, and press. Sew the bias strip to the front bottom curve of the skirt wedge, matching raw edges and using a ¼" seam allowance. Press the binding to the back side and pin so that the pressed edge slightly covers the stitched seam line. With thread that matches the binding, stitch in the ditch from the right side through all layers, catching the folded edge of the binding in the back. Complete this step for all of the wedges.

3. Make 4 units, each composed of 2 wedges, by sewing pairs of wedges together with a ½" seam, matching the bias edge with any pattern on the fabric (see photo). Press the seam open, and finish the seam by serging, covering it with seam tape, or topstitching through all layers ¼" to each side of the seam.

4. Select 2 units to form the sides of the skirt opening. These units will be numbered #1 and #4. (Numbering is clockwise from the opening of the tree skirt.) On the side of each unit that will be used for the opening, press the raw edge to the back ¼", press under again ¼", and topstitch from the wrong side through all layers ¼" from the edge. If you wish, make 6 ties from the remaining binding or plaid skirt fabric. Cut the strips 9½" by 1¼". Press the long edges to the center ¼".

    Fold the pressed edges together lengthwise and press again. Topstitch close to the pressed edges to complete the ties. Attach a pair of ties just above the binding on the outer hemmed edges of the 2 units, and a pair 16" above them. Reserve the last pair for the trunk edge, to be placed inside the bias facing as part of step 10.

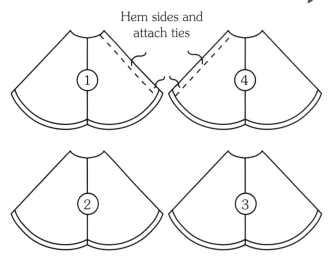

Hem sides and
attach ties

1  4

2  3

5. Trace the appliqué patterns onto fusible paper-backed web, then iron onto the chosen fabric. Trace 4 copies of the cow, then trace 4 more with each of the other two tails substituted for variation; you need a total of 12 cows. Cut out appliqué pieces. Remove the paper backing and fuse the pieces in place, following the placement diagram on the wedge pattern piece. **Do not fuse the large trees yet, except for the one placed on unit #4**. The large tree that would cover the seam at the skirt opening can be cut in half and applied to each side of the opening (half on unit #1 and half on unit #4), or the other trees on the left side of unit #4 can be shifted to allow room for this entire large tree on the right side opening. In either option, the large tree for this area can be applied now.

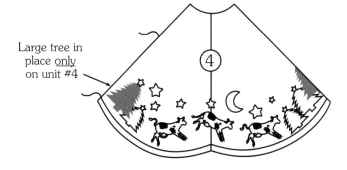

Large tree in place only on unit #4

6. Blanket stitch the cows using black thread, and satin stitch the other appliqué shapes,

using the co-ordinating threads. By machine, when satin stitching the trees, stars, and moon, use an iron-on fusible stabilizer on the back of the skirt, behind the shapes, to prevent stitch distortion and fabric stretching. Use matching green thread on the trees, pink on the udder bags, metallic gold on the gold stars, moons, and all the teats, metallic red on the red stars, and metallic pink on the pink star. **Use a longer stitch length on the lamé, to avoid cutting through the fabric.** Taper each bottom end of the teats to a point. Tear away the stabilizer from the wrong side of the skirt section as each area is completed.

7. Sew unit #2 to the left side of unit #1. Finish the seam, referring to Step 3, using your preferred method. Iron on the large tree and its star, overlapping the seam and satin-stitching it in place.

8. Repeat Step 7 for unit #3 and #4, sewing unit #3 to the right side of unit #4.

9. Sew the two halves of the tree skirt together, and add the final large tree and its star.

10. To finish the inner curve of the tree skirt, cut 1¼" x 44" bias strip from remaining skirt fabric. Press one short end of the strip ½" to the wrong side. With right sides facing and matching the pressed end of the strip to one end of the inner circle, pin the strip along the inner circle edge. Trim the raw short end of the strip ½" beyond the circle end, and press back. Stitch, using a ¼" seam allowance, then clip. Press the bias strip to the back of the skirt. Press the long raw edge of the strip under ¼" and pin in place. Insert the tree skirt ties at the circle ends, between the pressed strip and the tree skirt. Working from the back of the skirt, topstitch ¼" from the pressed strip edge, sewing through all layers. Be sure to catch the tie ends in this seam.

11. Cut ribbon into twelve 11" lengths. Tie ribbons into 2½" bows, and notch the ribbon ends. Seal with Fray Check to prevent raveling. Sew the loops of the bells under the bow knots and then attach them to each cow, as indicated on the pattern.

♥ Because I was a peeker as a child, and therefore ruined many a surprise for myself, I have chosen not to place family gifts under the tree prior to Christmas Eve after the children (now all teenagers) are tucked into their beds. Therefore, a tree skirt plays a major decorative role under our tree from Thanksgiving weekend until Christmas Day. Unfortunately, most tree skirts are too small for the noble fir that we traditionally purchase. My goal was to offer a very large skirt with designs on the edge to show beyond the branches of our family tree. I think you will agree that I accomplished this! We decorate our tree with the usual stuff: white mini-lights, glass bulbs, candy canes, etc. We also include "crackers," a British tradition I learned as a child living near London. These are cardboard tubes decorated with red and green paper and Christmas stickers, filled with a tissue-paper hat, a small toy, and a printed fortune. To open one, you pull a paper fuse, creating a loud snap. On Christmas Day, with invited family and friends, we place these crackers at each person's place and open them at the start of our mid-day dinner. Fortunes are read, hats are worn, and toys are admired, shared, and traded. Frequently, Christmas dinner features a honey-glazed spiral-cut ham which is devoured enthusiastically. All the teenagers know that the left-over ham and bone will be used to make authentic German lentil soup. It is this recipe I share with you.

# Linsensuppe
## (German Lentil Soup)

1 pound of lentils
½ pound of bacon, diced
2 medium onions, sliced
2 medium carrots, diced
2 quarts of water
1 cup of diced celery
2 tsp. salt

½ tsp. ground black pepper
½ tsp. dried thyme
2 bay leaves
l large potato, pared
1 ham bone
2 tbsp. fresh lemon juice

1. Wash the lentils. (Soak them overnight in cold water if necessary. Read the package label, as most lentils do not need to soak.)
2. Drain the lentils. In a large stock pot, sauté bacon until crisp. Add sliced onions and diced carrots, and continue sautéing until onions are golden.
3. Add lentils, water, sliced celery, salt, pepper, thyme, and bay leaves.
4. With a medium grater, grate the pared potato into the lentil mixture. Add the ham bone.
5. Simmer covered for 3 hours. Lentils should be tender. Remove the bay leaves.
6. Remove the ham bone and cut all meat from bone. Discard the bone, and return the meat to the pot.
7. To serve at once, add lemon juice. To eat later, refrigerate or freeze without adding lemon juice. Yield: 9½ cups of hearty soup.

# JEAN WELLS

## Christmas Mini-Socks and Tree Skirt

*Jean Wells has been my other role model throughout my career, and how wonderful to present her in the same book with Yvonne Porcella! She is always there to listen, to guide, to encourage everyone, someone to whom even the other professionals turn for help. Jean is the author of more than a dozen books, the owner of The Stitchin' Post in Sisters, Oregon, a teacher and lecturer, a member of the advisory council for Quilt Market — and on the second weekend of July every year she directs the most unbelievable quilt show. Imagine being in a town of the Old West, complete with wooden sidewalks and snowcapped mountains — and the front of every building hung with quilts! Had it not been for Jean, my first book, Christmas Traditions from the Heart, would never have been born: thanks to her frequent "just do it," here I am, doing it again!*

These mini-socks and tree skirt are perfect for gifts. Fill a sock with small remembrances for a special person. Hang them from a garland on the mantle, put them on the Christmas tree, or use them as table favors. The small tree skirt was designed for a table-top tree, but you can easily enlarge it: just cut a larger square to start with, and enlarge the appliqué shapes on a photocopier.

To decorate the socks and skirt, fuse appliqués with paper-backed adhesive, then use a buttonhole stitch around them. Read the paper-backed adhesive package carefully first, so you buy one that can be stitched through. I prefer the film type, which adheres evenly and takes a stitch easily. Be careful to avoid too much heat, or the adhesive will melt and penetrate the fabric. You can stitch by hand, as I have done, or use the buttonhole stitch on a machine; if you use a machine, use a thread that is heavy enough for the stitches to show.

## Christmas Mini-Socks

### Materials Needed

- ¼ yard of a lively monochromatic print fabric for each sock
- ⅛ yard each of 3 co-ordinating fabrics for appliqués
- ¼ yard of sewable paper-backed adhesive
- 1 skein of black 6-strand embroidery floss
- 6" of black ⅜"-wide black ribbon for hanger

## Assembly

1. Fold the sock fabric in half with short ends together, then end-to-end again into quarters. Place the sock pattern on the four thicknesses. Cut out the sock.

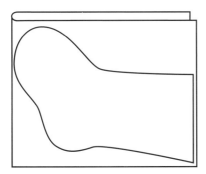

You will have two lining pieces and a front and a back. Use ¼" seam allowance when sewing the fabric: the seam allowance is included in the pattern.

2. Trace the appliqués you want to use onto the paper side of the adhesive. (Remember that the bird will reverse direction.) Trim around the appliqués, leaving ¼" of paper beyond each shape. Fuse the appliqués to the wrong sides of the pieces of fabric. Cut out on the pencil lines.

3. Peel the paper from the appliqués and decoratively arrange them on the sock front. Remember that ¼" of the sock edge will be lost for the seam allowance. Match the straight edge of the border to the top of the sock. Fuse the appliqués in place.

4. Following the diagram for buttonhole stitching and using two strands of floss if stitching by hand, stitch around the appliqués.

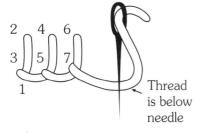

If working on the sewing machine, sew around the appliqués. Do not buttonhole stitch the straight edge of the top border. When you come to a sharp point, pull the thread to the back, then bring it up again close to where you pulled it through; this will keep the thread from turning on itself.

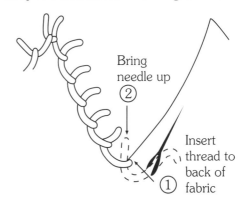

For the appliqué circles, crisscross twice and tack the center.

5. Place the appliquéd sock front and the matching lining piece together, right sides facing. Sew across the top of the sock, ¼" from the edge. Press the seam open and the lining to the back, with the wrong sides facing. Do the same with the sock back and remaining lining.

6. Place the sock pieces together, with the right sides of the sock front and back facing. Stitch around the edges of the sock, ¼" from the edge, leaving the top open. Clip the curves as shown.

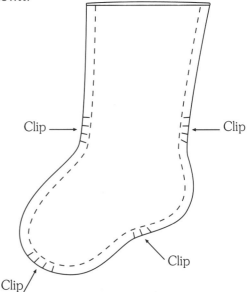

Turn to the right side and press lightly. Buttonhole stitch around the *edges* of the sock, except for the top.

7. Fold the ribbon in half and turn the raw edges under ¼". Tack the ribbon loop to the back of the sock by hand.

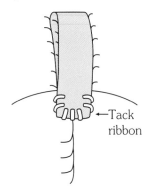

←Tack ribbon

# Tree Skirt

## Materials Needed

- ⅔ yard of a lively monochromatic print fabric for the skirt
- ¼ yard of a co-ordinating fabric for border
- ⅛ yard of a co-ordinating fabric for circles and bird wings
- ¼ yard of a co-ordinating fabric for stars and bird bodies
- 1 yard of sewable paper-backed adhesive
- 24"-square of thin, lightweight batting
- 1 skein of black 6-strand embroidery floss
- 1½ yards of ⅜"-wide black ribbon for ties

## Assembly

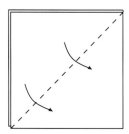

1. Cut a 20" square of the main fabric. Fold it in quarters, then once more, to create a wedge.

Mark a curve 10" from the point, and cut on this line.

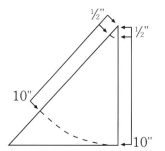

Measure and cut a hole ½" from the point for the tree trunk.

2. Cut a slit from the outer edge of the skirt to the inside hole. Using this piece of fabric as a pattern, cut the lining from the remaining main fabric.

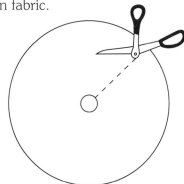

3. Trace eight circles, nine borders, and four birds, wings, and stars onto the paper side of the adhesive. Repeat Step 2 of the Christmas Mini-Socks with the co-ordinating fabrics.

4. Arrange the border pieces around the skirt, matching the edges, and overlapping where necessary. Fuse them in place. Remember that ¼" of the skirt edge will be lost for the seam allowance. Arrange the birds, stars, and circles on the skirt, and fuse them.

5. Buttonhole stitch around the appliqués, following the directions given in Step 4 of the Christmas Mini-Socks. Do not appliqué the bottom of the borders.

6. Place the skirt and lining right sides together and cover with the batting. Pin the layers together. Sew around the edges, ¼" from the edge, leaving a 3" opening. Trim the excess batting and clip the curves. Turn to the right side through the opening. Lightly press. Close the opening with small stitches.

7. Cut six 5" lengths of ribbon and turn under one end of each. Tack the turned end of three ribbons to the wrong side of the skirt at the top, middle, and bottom of the slit.

Repeat for the opposite side of the slit, and trim the ribbon tails diagonally. Tie ribbons into bows.

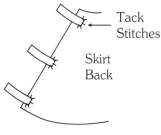

←Tack Stitches

Skirt Back

❤ Set your Christmas table with a small decorated tree as the centerpiece, of course using the tree skirt. Place a mini-sock on each plate to hold the flatware — and to serve as a favor for each guest to keep. You might also want to include in each sock a copy of the dessert recipe: it makes a great change from pumpkin pie.

# Pumpkin Squares

**For the crust, combine**
1¾ cups of crushed graham crackers
⅓ cup of sugar
½ cup of melted margarine.
Press the mixture into the bottom of a 9" x 13" pan.

**Beat together, until light and fluffy,**
2 eggs
¾ cup of sugar
8 ounces of softened cream cheese.
Pour this mixture over the crust and bake at 350° for 20 minutes, then let cool.

**In a double boiler, combine**
16 ounces of canned pumpkin
3 egg yolks
½ cup of sugar
½ cup of milk
1 teaspoon of salt
2 teaspoons of cinnamon.
Cook on medium heat about 5 minutes, until it is thick, and set it aside.

**In a small saucepan, sprinkle**
1 package of gelatin on
¼ cup of water.
Stir over low heat until the gelatin powder has dissolved. Stir it into the pumpkin mixture and let it cool.

Beat the remaining egg whites until they are foamy, then gradually add
¼ cup of sugar.
Fold this into the cooled pumpkin mixture and pour it over the filling. Refrigerate for several hours. This can be topped with whipped cream, if you wish.

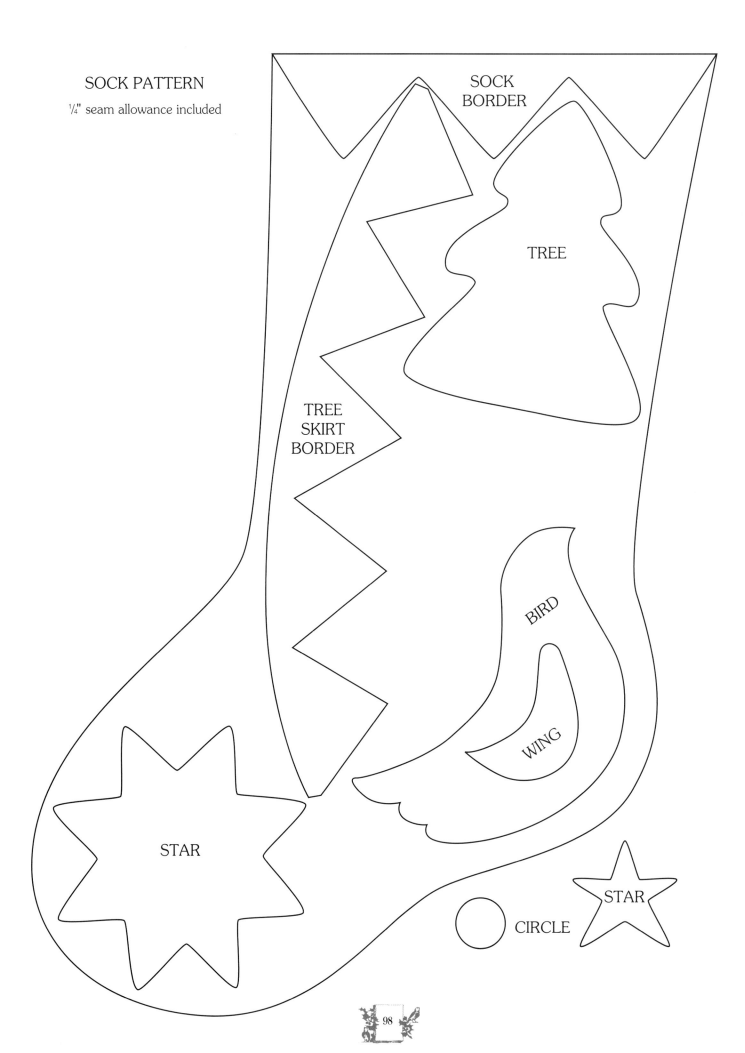

SOCK PATTERN
¼" seam allowance included

SOCK
BORDER

TREE

TREE
SKIRT
BORDER

BIRD

WING

STAR

STAR

CIRCLE

# ROSE SHEIFER

*Of all the dear friends I'm sharing with you in this book, Rose Sheifer is the most recent. We first met when C&T Publishing chose her, because of the splendid work she had already done for them, to do the illustrations and design for* Christmas Traditions from the Heart. *My first book could never have happened so easily, nor so beautifully, had she not brought so much talent and warmth and understanding to its creation. She has shared with me so much of her time, her knowledge, and her laughter. Now she shares with you her stunning design for a frame for your Christmas letters, which you can share with your loved ones, as well as a design for special recipe cards for your permanent files.*

## Holiday Letter and Recipe Cards

### Holiday Letter

Make several sharp, clean photocopies of the artwork — spares for practice and mistakes. (You will want to place a piece of white paper in the center to mask out the recipe card.) Transfer your letter onto a copy by hand, typewriter, or computer output to a laser printer (making sure you have allowed margins for the artwork).

Take this master letter to your local photocopy center. Make your copies on a high-quality machine to insure the best reproduction. You can choose from a wide selection of papers, such as parchment, linen or laid finish, recycled, vellum. Many colors and textures are also available. Consider buying a stationery pack with matching envelopes. You can also use card stock and fold it down as a self-mailer.

If you wish, you can color these copies with colored pencils, pastel pencils, regular or metallic markers (use thin tips). Avoid water-based materials, as they will tend to buckle the paper.

### Recipe Card

Make 4 photocopies of the card and lay them out on an 8½" x 11" sheet of paper. Photocopy the sheet onto white or colored card stock, then cut the recipe cards apart. They will be the correct size to fit into a standard index card box.

♥ For me, Christmas is my memories of childhood celebrations with my family. Every year my brothers, uncles, aunts, grandfather, cousins, and nieces gathered for an enormous feast. Italians love to eat and talk, and our family was no exception. Christmas day was a joyous time for us because we sat around the table for hours, savoring one dish after another while we argued and laughed.

My mother would start food preparation two days before Christmas. She is a marvelous Italian cook who prepares her sumptuous dishes without recipes. Her hands are the measuring cups and her fingers the measuring spoons. It all came together by memory, spontaneity, and intuition. Of all the delicious food my mother prepared, her stuffed mushrooms are still among my favorites. But please, follow her advice if you make this recipe: "To get the best results, always use the *finest* and *freshest* ingredients."

## Mrs. Schiafone's Stuffed Mushrooms

1 lb. large white or brown crimini mushrooms
1 large clove garlic, chopped fine
⅓ cup of onion, chopped fine
1½ tbsp. of olive oil
1 tbsp. of unsalted butter
½ cup of Italian-style bread crumbs
½ cup of grated imported Asiago
   or Parmesan cheese

1 tbsp. of minced fresh basil or ½ tbsp.
   of dried basil
1½ tbsp. of minced fresh parsley or
   ¾ tbsp. of dried parsley
Freshly ground black pepper, to taste,
   if desired
¼ cup of grated mozzarella cheese

Wipe the mushrooms clean with a dampened paper towel. Remove the stems and discard the ends. Chop the stems finely. Heat the olive oil and butter in a non-stick frying pan. Add onions and sauté over medium heat for 2 minutes. Add mushroom stems and garlic and saute another 2 minutes. Turn the heat off. Add bread crumbs, basil, parsley, Asiago or Parmesan cheese, and pepper.

Lightly oil a glass baking dish. Brush a little olive oil all around the outside of each mushroom top. Pack each mushroom with a heap of the stuffing, pressing it down firmly with the rounded side of a teaspoon. The stuffing should be in a mound. Place the mushrooms stuffing up in the baking dish. Top each with some grated mozzarella.

Bake uncovered in a 350° preheated oven for 20 to 25 minutes. Serve hot. *Buon appetito!*

*Season's Greetings*

Margaret Peters has been a craftswoman all her life. Her real involvement with fiber arts began in 1975, when she started to create needlepoint designs — and to win national awards for them. Teaching at and managing a needlepoint store, and then representing needlepoint and cross-stitch manufacturers, she attended trade shows; she became fascinated by the quilting she encountered and began representing quilting suppliers as well. Eventually, she carried the products of 75 pattern and fabric companies.

By the mid-1980's, she had also begun to design her own dolls, and was nationally known for her Christmas shows for her clients. These talents came together in 1987, when she was invited to design a Christmas tree for the Smithsonian Institution. She then started her own design and supply company, and she was asked to create dolls for Fairfield Processing and touring shows: Dollmakers Magic, Cut from the Same Cloth, Accessories as Art, etc. She began national touring herself, speaking especially to quilt and antique audiences — including three times at Quilt Market and Quilt Festival — about the Smithsonian experience, effective store displays, and Christmas. In 1991, she was invited by West Point Pepperell to design a promotion for their fabrics: she created Old Glory: Long May She Wave, the flag challenge which has toured the country. Her first book, *Christmas Traditions from the Heart,* was published by C&T Publishing in 1992.

Her home in Walnut Creek, California, is such a treasure trove of antiques, American crafts, patriotic memorabilia, and Christmas crafts that it receives media coverage regularly, it is used by book publishers for photographic settings, and it is the site of annual Christmas tours by various crafts organizations.

Margaret's line of roving for doll hair is marketed under the name Ewe and Me Roving; her American flags by the yard, angels and other Christmas ornaments are marketed as Long May She Wave. Both are available in your local craft shops. You may obtain further information and her catalogue from: Margaret Peters; Department I; 325 Lancaster Road; Walnut Creek, CA 94595.

MARGARET PETERS

# Other Fine Quilting Books
# From C&T Publishing

*An Amish Adventure*, Roberta Horton

*Appliqué 12 Easy Ways!* Elly Sienkiewicz

*The Art of Silk Ribbon Embroidery*, Judith Montano

*Baltimore Album Quilts, Historic Notes and Antique Patterns*, Elly Sienkiewicz

*Baltimore Beauties and Beyond* (2 Volumes), Elly Sienkiewicz

*The Best From Gooseberry Hill: Patterns For Stuffed Animals & Dolls*, Kathy Pace

*Boston Commons Quilt*, Blanche Young and Helen Young Frost

*Calico and Beyond*, Roberta Horton

*A Celebration of Hearts*, Jean Wells and Marina Anderson

*A Colorful Book*, Yvonne Porcella

*Christmas Traditions from the Heart*, Margaret Peters

*Crazy Quilt Handbook*, Judith Montano

*Crazy Quilt Odyssey*, Judith Montano

*Design a Baltimore Album Quilt!* Elly Sienkiewicz

*Dimensional Appliqué—Baskets, Blooms & Borders*, Elly Sienkiewicz

*Dollmaking with Polymer and Paper Clays: Ideas and Techniques*, Susanna Oroyan

*Flying Geese Quilt*, Blanche Young and Helen Young Frost

*14,287 Pieces of Fabrics and Other Poems*, Jean Ray Laury

*Friendship's Offering*, Susan McKelvey

*Happy Trails*, Pepper Cory

*Heirloom Machine Quilting*, Harriet Hargrave

*Imagery on Fabric*, Jean Ray Laury

*Irish Chain Quilt*, Blanche Young and Helen Young Frost

*Isometric Perspective*, Katie Pasquini-Masopust

*Landscapes & Illusions*, Joen Wolfrom

*Let's Make Waves*, Marianne Fons and Liz Porter

*The Magical Effects of Color*, Joen Wolfrom

*Mariner's Compass*, Judy Mathieson

*Mastering Machine Appliqué*, Harriet Hargrave

*Memorabilia Quilting*, Jean Wells

*The New Lone Star Handbook*, Blanche Young and Helen Young Frost

*NSA Series: Bloomin' Creations*, Jean Wells

*NSA Series: Holiday Magic*, Jean Wells

*NSA Series: Hometown*, Jean Wells

*NSA Series: Fans, Hearts, & Folk Art*, Jean Wells

*Pattern Play*, Doreen Speckmann

*Perfect Pineapples*, Jane Hall and Dixie Haywood

*Picture This*, Jean Wells and Marina Anderson

*Pieced Clothing*, Yvonne Porcella

*Pieced Clothing Variations*, Yvonne Porcella

*Plaids and Stripes*, Roberta Horton

*PQME Series: Basket Quilt*, Jean Wells

*PQME Series: Bear's Paw Quilt*, Jean Wells

*PQME Series: Country Bunny Quilt*, Jean Wells

*PQME Series: Milky Way Quilt*, Jean Wells

*PQME Series: Nine-Patch Quilt*, Jean Wells

*PQME Series: Pinwheel Quilt*, Jean Wells

*PQME Series: Sawtooth Star Quilt*, Jean Wells

*PQME Series: Stars & Hearts Quilt*, Jean Wells

*Quilts, Quilts, and More Quilts!* Diana McClun and Laura Nownes

*Recollections*, Judith Montano

*Stitching Free: Easy Machine Pictures*, Shirley Nilsson

*Story Quilts*, Mary Mashuta

*Symmetry: A Design System for Quiltmakers*, Ruth B. McDowell

*3 Dimensional Design*, Katie Pasquini

*A Treasury of Quilt Labels*, Susan McKelvey

*Trip Around the World Quilts*, Blanche Young and Helen Young Frost

*Visions: The Art of the Quilt*, Quilt San Diego

*Whimsical Animals*, Miriam Gourley

*Wearable Art for Real People*, Mary Mashuta

For more information write for a free catalog from
C & T Publishing
P.O. Box 1456
Lafayette, CA 94549
(1-800-284-1114)

Christmas joy is in my heart